BY THE EDITORS OF CONSUMER GUIDE®

FAVORITE *Oriental* **BRAND NAME RECIPES**

BEEKMAN HOUSE
New York

Contents

1985 edition published by Beekman House
Distributed by Crown Publishers, Inc.
225 Park Avenue South
New York, New York 10003

ISBN 0-517-60410-8

Manufactured in the United States of America
h g f e d c b a

COVER RECIPES

Front Cover:
Left: "Saucy Stir-Fried Shrimp"
Borden Inc.
Right: "Wheat Germ Egg Rolls"
International Multifoods
Back Cover:
Left: "Chicken with Broccoli and Walnuts"
La Choy Food Products
Right: "Chinese Almond Cookies"
"Almond Won Ton Cookies"
Almond Board of California

Cover Design: Linda Snow Shum

Introduction

This book brings you a marvelous collection of *your* favorite Oriental recipes—the ones you remember from food packages, boxtops, labels and advertisements. Hundreds of recipes for Oriental dishes—including several for egg rolls and spring rolls and various kinds of chop suey, fried rice and chow mein—are here at your fingertips. You can choose from a variety of sweet-and-sour dishes or foo-yung recipes. If you like to stir fry, you'll be delighted with the selection of meats, fish, chicken and vegetables you can make using this quick and easy cooking method.

Everything is combined into one fantastic volume for your Oriental cooking pleasure—appetizers, soups, salads, main dishes, vegetables and other side dishes, and even desserts. You can easily create a complete Oriental meal.

From quick-and-easy to elegant, there's a recipe to suit every need. Get ready to serve your family and friends such delicious favorites as Egg Drop Soup, Teriyaki Meat Sticks, Japanese Stir Fry Fish, Pepper Steak, Tempura, Meatball Sukiyaki, Almond Won Ton Cookies, and so many more!

An easy-to-use INDEX is provided so that you can locate a recipe by its title, by the brand name product used in the recipe, or by the main food ingredient, such as "chicken."

For your convenience, an address directory of all food manufacturers listed in the book has also been included (see ACKNOWLEDGMENTS). The recipes in this book are reprinted exactly as they appear on the food packages or in the advertisements. Any questions or comments regarding the recipes should be directed to the individual manufacturers for prompt attention. All of the recipes have been copyrighted by the food manufacturers and cannot be reprinted without their permission. By printing these recipes, CONSUMER GUIDE® is *not* endorsing particular brand name foods.

Appetizers

Christian Brothers®

Ginger Pork Balls in Sherry-Orange Sauce

1 large slice white bread, crumbled (about 1 cup crumbs)
¼ cup **THE CHRISTIAN BROTHERS® Golden Sherry**
1½ pounds lean ground pork
½ cup minced water chestnuts
2 tablespoons soy sauce
1 egg yolk
2 teaspoons ground ginger
1 large clove garlic, crushed
Sherry-Orange Sauce*

In large bowl combine bread and sherry; set aside 10 minutes. Add remaining ingredients except Sherry-Orange Sauce. Mix to blend thoroughly. Cover and chill at least 30 minutes. Form into 1-inch balls. Place slightly apart on baking sheet. Bake in 400 degree oven about 20 minutes until cooked through and lightly browned.

Meanwhile prepare Sherry-Orange Sauce. Add drained pork balls to sauce. Cook over medium heat until hot through, stirring gently. Remove from heat; gently stir in orange segments (reserved in Sherry-Orange Sauce recipe). Serve hot with cocktail picks for spearing. *Makes about 5 dozen*

*Sherry-Orange Sauce

2 cans (11 ounces *each*) mandarin orange segments
Chicken broth or bouillon (about ¾ cup)
⅓ cup **THE CHRISTIAN BROTHERS® Golden Sherry**
2 tablespoons *each* cornstarch and soy sauce

Drain liquid from orange segments into 2-cup measure; reserve segments. Add broth to orange liquid to make 2 cups. Pour into 2-quart saucepan. Mix sherry, cornstarch and soy sauce; add to saucepan. Cook and stir over medium heat until smooth and thickened. Simmer 1 minute.

First Prize winner **THE CHRISTIAN BROTHERS®** contest

Holiday Meatballs

¾ cup **3-MINUTE BRAND® Oats** (either old fashioned or quick) or 2 packets **Regular Flavor HARVEST BRAND®** Instant Oatmeal
1½ pounds ground beef
2 15¼ ounce cans crushed pineapple packed in juice, drained (reserve juice)
⅓ cup finely chopped onion
¼ cup finely chopped green pepper
2 eggs
1½ teaspoons salt
¼ teaspoon ground ginger
¼ cup cornstarch
½ cup brown sugar
⅔ cup vinegar
2 tablespoons soy sauce
½ cup chopped green pepper

Combine oats, ground beef, ½ cup of the drained pineapple, onion, ¼ cup green pepper, eggs, salt, and ginger; mix well. Shape into 1-inch meatballs. Place on 15 × 10 × 1-inch baking sheet. Bake in a 350°F oven about 15 minutes or till done, turning once.

Meanwhile, in saucepan combine cornstarch and brown sugar. Add water to reserved pineapple juice to make 2 cups liquid. Add liquid, vinegar, and soy sauce to cornstarch mixture, stirring till smooth. Cook, stirring constantly, till thickened and bubbly; cook and stir 1 to 2 minutes more. Stir in the ½ cup chopped green pepper and remaining drained pineapple. Heat through. Stir in hot meatballs. (We suggest a chafing dish or fondue pot for serving.) *Makes 5 dozen appetizers*

Note: Meatballs may be served over rice or pasta for a delicious main dish. You can make these ahead, refrigerate, and reheat for serving.

Sweet and Sour Meatballs

2 lb. ground beef (lean)
1 cup apple sauce
½ cup bread crumbs
1 egg

Combine these ingredients and form meatballs. In large pot, add:

1 12 oz. bottle chili sauce
¼ cup **NOILLY PRAT Sweet**
12 oz. water
¼ cup grape jam
Drop of lemon juice

Bring sauce to boil, drop in meatballs and simmer for ½ hour.

Seafood Spring Rolls

1 can (12½ oz.) **BUMBLE BEE® Chunk Light Tuna***
1 cup vegetable oil
½ cup chopped green onion
1 carrot, shredded
½ cup slivered almonds
2 cups bean sprouts
1 tablespoon soy sauce
¼ teaspoon pepper
¼ teaspoon ground ginger
1 package (1 lb.) egg roll skins
Water
Soy sauce for dipping

Drain tuna. Heat 1 tablespoon oil in skillet. Sauté green onion, carrots, almonds and bean sprouts. Add soy sauce, pepper and ginger. Cook, stirring several minutes. Remove from heat and fold in tuna. Place two rounded tablespoons of mixture on the diagonal of each skin. Tuck flap pointing towards you in. Fold in sides. Roll up, sealing with water. Heat remaining oil in shallow 7-inch skillet. Deep fry about 30 seconds on each side or until golden. Serve with soy sauce. *Makes 26 servings*

*Or use 2 cans (6½ oz. each) **BUMBLE BEE® Chunk Light Tuna**

Chinese Spring Rolls

1 can (1 lb., 4 oz.) **DOLE® Crushed Pineapple,** drained
1 can (4 oz.) diced water chestnuts, drained
⅓ cup chopped green onions
1 can (1 lb.) bean sprouts, drained
2 cans (4 oz. ea.) deveined shrimp, drained, or ¾ lb. fresh cooked shrimp
2 cans (8 oz. ea.) refrigerated crescent rolls
Soy sauce

Combine pineapple, water chestnuts, onions and bean sprouts. Chop and fold in shrimp. Open one can refrigerated rolls. Unroll dough. Separate into 4 rectangles. Pinch diagonal separations together. Roll each rectangle on lightly floured board to 7 inches x 9 inches. Cut each rectangle into 3 strips 7 inches x 3 inches each. Spoon one heaping tablespoon filling into center of each strip, spreading lengthwise. Moisten edges with water. Roll dough over filling lengthwise. Press open ends with tines of a fork. Remove to lightly greased cooky sheet. Repeat with second can of rolls. Bake at 375° for 15 to 20 minutes. Slice each diagonally into 3 bite-size rolls. Serve hot with soy sauce and dunk if desired.
Makes 72 hors d' oeuvres

Glaze: Brush with beaten whole egg if desired before baking.

Wheat Germ Egg Rolls

1 cup bean sprouts, coarsely chopped
¾ cup **KRETSCHMER Regular Wheat Germ**
½ cup grated carrot
½ cup green onion, cut into 1½-inch pieces
½ cup minced water chestnuts
3 Tbsp. soy sauce
2 Tbsp. dry sherry
1 tsp. grated ginger root
12 egg roll skins
1 tsp. cornstarch
3 Tbsp. water

Combine . . . all ingredients *except* egg roll skins, cornstarch and water. Mix well.

Wrap . . . . . . skins in damp paper toweling, taking out one at a time.

Place . . . . . . ¼ cup filling on each skin. Cover half the skin, leaving a narrow border along bottom and side edges.

Fold . . . . . . narrow edge up over filling. Fold in side edges. Roll to within ½ inch of top edge.

Brush . . . . . top edge with cornstarch mixed with water. Seal well. Cover with damp paper toweling.

Heat . . . . . . oil (about 3 inches deep) to 350°.

Fry . . . . egg rolls, a few at a time, about 3 minutes until golden.

Drain . . . . . . well. Cut each roll diagonally into 3 pieces. Serve hot. *Makes 3 dozen appetizers*

Gerber®

Egg Rolls

1 small head cabbage, finely shredded (about 4 cups)
1 cup chopped celery
1 cup diced green onion
1 can (28 oz.) bean sprouts, rinsed and drained
3 chicken bouillon cubes
3 cups water
4 eggs, beaten
2 tablespoons soy sauce
1 jar (4½ oz.) **GERBER® Strained Carrots**
2 jars (3½ oz. each) **GERBER® Strained Chicken**
1 package (16 oz.) egg roll wrappers
Corn starch
Water

In large mixing bowl, place shredded cabbage, celery, green onions, and bean sprouts. Cover with water. Salt lightly and set aside for one hour. Drain.

In large saucepan, place bouillon cubes in 3 cups water. Add drained vegetables. Boil until vegetables go limp. Drain again.

Mix together eggs and soy sauce. Pour over drained vegetables. Stir well and boil two more minutes. Cool. Add chicken and carrots. Mix well. Salt and pepper to taste. (If any liquid remains in bowl, drain before filling wrappers.) Put about 2 heaping tablespoons of the filling in the center of each egg roll wrapper. Roll. Seal edges with a water and corn starch mixture. Deep fat fry to a golden brown. Serve with either Sweet-n-Sour Sauce* or Plum Sauce.**   *Yield: 18 egg rolls*

VARIATION:

For appetizers follow above recipe using 1 package (16 oz.) wonton skins.   *Yield: 50 small egg rolls*

*Sweet-n-Sour Sauce

½ cup brown sugar
3 tablespoons corn starch
2 jars (4.2 fl. oz. each) GERBER® Strained
  Orange-Pineapple Juice
⅓ cup vinegar
2 tablespoons soy sauce
1 teaspoon salt

Combine all ingredients in medium saucepan. Stir over medium heat until bubbly.   *Yield: Approximately 1½ cups sauce*

**Plum Sauce

2 jars (4¾ oz. each) GERBER® Strained Plums With
  Tapioca
¼ cup brown sugar, packed
¼ cup catsup
1½ tablespoons vinegar

Combine all ingredients in medium saucepan. Stir over medium heat until bubbly.   *Yield: Approximately 1⅓ cups sauce*

Spicy Cocktail Dip

1 bottle chili sauce (12 oz.)
2 Tbsp. lemon juice
2 Tbsp. salad oil
1 Tbsp. cider vinegar
2 tsp. brown sugar
1 tsp. dehydrated onion flakes
½ tsp. dry mustard
½ tsp. hot pepper sauce
½ tsp. salt

Combine ingredients in saucepan, heat to boiling and simmer 5 minutes. Serve with **JENO'S**® Egg Rolls.   *Makes 1¼ cups*

Creamy Mustard Dip

1 cup mayonnaise
3 tsp. dry mustard
1 tsp. cider vinegar
1 tsp. finely chopped onion
½ tsp. prepared horseradish

Combine ingredients and chill. Serve with **JENO'S**® Egg Rolls.   *Makes 1 cup*

Sweet-Sour Dip

Mix ⅓ cup pineapple, apricot or peach preserves, ⅓ cup tomato catsup and 1 Tbsp. vinegar. Add soy sauce to taste and contents of mustard packet. Serve with **JENO'S**® Egg Rolls.   *Makes ⅔ cup*

Sour Cream Teriyaki Dip

¼ tsp. ground ginger
¼ tsp. garlic powder
3 Tbsp. soy sauce
½ cup sour cream

Combine ingredients and let stand a few minutes before serving. Serve with **JENO'S**® Egg Rolls.   *Makes ¾ cup*

Mazola®

Teriyaki Kabobs

1 pound chicken breasts, boned, skinned, cut into 36
  cubes
1 can (20 oz.) pineapple chunks, well-drained
1 large green pepper, cut into 36 pieces
¼ cup MAZOLA® Corn Oil
¼ cup KARO® Dark Corn Syrup
¼ cup soy sauce
¼ cup sliced green onion
¼ cup sesame seed
¼ teaspoon dry mustard
¼ teaspoon pepper

In shallow baking dish place chicken, pineapple and green pepper. In small bowl stir together corn oil, corn syrup, soy sauce, green onion, sesame seed, mustard and pepper until well mixed. Pour over chicken mixture; toss to coat evenly. Cover; refrigerate several hours or overnight. Arrange green pepper, chicken and pineapple on 36 wooden picks. Baste with some of remaining sauce. Broil 4 inches from source of heat 2 to 3 minutes, turning and basting once, or until chicken is cooked through.   *Makes 36*

Menehune Chicken

24 chicken wings
1 cup KIKKOMAN Soy Sauce
¾ cup finely chopped green onions & tops
⅓ cup sugar
4 teaspoons vegetable oil
1 clove garlic, crushed
1½ teaspoons ground ginger *or* 1 tablespoon fresh
  ginger root

Disjoint chicken wings; discard tips. Blend soy sauce, green onions, sugar, oil, garlic and ginger in large mixing bowl. Add chicken pieces; cover and marinate 30 minutes. Remove chicken; reserve marinade. Place chicken, side by side, in shallow baking pan, skin side down. Bake, uncovered in 350°F oven 15 minutes. Turn pieces; baste with marinade and bake 15 minutes longer.   *Makes about 4 dozen appetizers*

COOKIN' GOOD™
GRADE A CHICKEN

Teriyaki Tidbits

14 COOKIN' GOOD™ Chicken Wings (about 3 lb.)

Marinade:
1 cup teriyaki sauce
½ cup molasses
½ cup lemon or lime juice
¼ cup honey
1 teaspoon of garlic powder or 1 clove fresh garlic, crushed
¼ cup instant onions, minced
1 cup vegetable oil
1 cup white wine
1 teaspoon paprika
Dipping sauce*

Disjoint wings, reserve tips for stock. In a large glass bowl, combine marinade ingredients. Add wing pieces and marinate at least four hours (preferably overnight).

CONVENTIONAL METHOD:
Preheat oven to 400 degrees. Drain marinade and reserve for basting and sauce recipe. Place wing pieces in a single layer in a shallow baking dish. Roast 35-45 minutes, basting often with marinade, until crisp and brown.

MICROWAVE METHOD:
Same as above except use a microwave baking dish. Microwave 12-15 minutes, full power, 650 watts. Baste and stir pieces often. Crisp under browning unit or conventional broiler.

*Dipping Sauce

2 teaspoons of cornstarch
1 cup of Marinade

Blend marinade and cornstarch together in a saucepan (without heat). Stirring constantly, bring the mixture to a boil over a medium heat until thick and bubbly. Serve this sauce with the Teriyaki Tidbits.

THE ORIGINAL WORCESTERSHIRE

Chicken Livers Hong Kong
(Low Calorie)

1 pound (about 12) chicken livers
1 can (8 oz.) water chestnuts, drained and halved
2 tablespoons **LEA & PERRINS Worcestershire Sauce**
1 tablespoon dry sherry
1 tablespoon soy sauce
1 teaspoon garlic powder
½ teaspoon salt
¼ teaspoon ground ginger

Cut chicken livers in half; place in a medium bowl. Stir in remaining ingredients. Cover and refrigerate for 1 hour. On wooden picks

skewer a piece of liver and a water chestnut half. Place on a rack in a broiler pan. Broil under a preheated hot broiler until cooked as desired, about 2 minutes on each side.

Calorie Count: About 58 calories per hors d'oeuvre

Chicken Kabobs
(Yakitori)

3 pounds chicken breasts
1 pound chicken livers
1 bunch green onions, cut into 1-inch lengths
1 cup **KIKKOMAN Soy Sauce**
¼ cup sugar
1 tablespoon salad oil
2 cloves garlic, crushed
¾ teaspoon ground ginger (OR 1 tablespoon grated fresh ginger root)

Skin and bone chicken, keeping meat in one piece; cut into 1-inch lengths. Thread bamboo skewers each with a chicken piece, a green onion piece, and a chicken liver piece. Blend together soy sauce, sugar, oil, garlic and ginger. Place kabobs in large shallow baking pan; pour sauce over. Brush each kabob thoroughly with sauce. Marinate about 1 hour and remove; reserve marinade. Broil 5 inches below preheated broiler 3 minutes on each side, brushing with reserved marinade after turning.

Makes about 4 dozen appetizers

Lipton.

South Seas Pork Tidbits

1 envelope **LIPTON® Onion Soup Mix**
3 tablespoons lime juice
2 tablespoons water
1 teaspoon ground ginger
1½ pounds boneless pork, thinly sliced and cut into 1-inch squares

In large shallow baking dish, blend onion soup mix, lime juice, water and ginger; add pork. Cover and marinate in refrigerator, turning occasionally, 4 hours or overnight.

Remove pork, reserving marinade. Thread pork on 6-inch skewers; brush with marinade. Broil, turning occasionally, 15 minutes or until done. *Makes about 6 dozen appetizers*

Adolph's®

Oriental Riblets

½ cup soy sauce
½ cup dry sherry
½ cup water
¼ cup brown sugar
2 tablespoons lemon juice
2 cloves garlic, crushed
1 capful **ADOLPH'S® 100% Natural Tenderizer—Seasoned**
2 pounds pork riblets, cut into individual ribs

In a large bowl, thoroughly blend first 7 ingredients. Add riblets, making certain marinade covers meat. Marinate 1 hour, turning occasionally. Broil 5 inches from heat about 8 minutes per side or until done.

Makes 6 servings as an appetizer

Won Ton with Sweet and Sour Sauce

1 pkg. won ton skins
¼ lb. ground pork or beef
1 Tbsp. soy sauce
Dash of salt and pepper
1 tsp. monosodium glutamate
4 Tbsp. finely chopped green onion
½ can (small) water chestnuts, chopped
Sauce*

Combine all ingredients except won ton skins in a skillet. Brown until there is no trace of pink in the meat. Lay 1 skin down and in the center place 1 Tbsp. of the meat mixture. With water and gentle pressure seal skin into the shape of a triangle. Fry in deep fat (400°) until golden brown.

*Sauce

Combine:
   ½ cup sugar
   1 cup MARUKAN® Rice
      Vinegar (Genuine Brewed)
   1 tsp. salt
   ¼ cup catsup

Bring to boil. Thicken with 1 Tbsp. cornstarch mixed with water to form a paste. Cook until thickened. If sauce is too strong, add water until you get the desired strength. Sliced onions and pineapple chunks may be added if desired.

PEPPERIDGE FARM®

Chinese Pork and Shrimp Pockets

1 package (17¼ ounces) PEPPERIDGE FARM®
   "Bake It Fresh" Frozen Puff Pastry
1 pound pork cutlets, cut into julienne strips
½ cup green onions or scallions, sliced
2 tablespoons vegetable oil
2 tablespoons soy sauce
1½ teaspoons ground ginger or 2 teaspoons grated
   fresh ginger root
10 ounces cooked baby shrimp, shelled and deveined
1 egg yolk mixed with 1 tablespoon water
Sweet and Sour Sauce*

Thaw puff pastry sheets for 20 minutes. In a large skillet, sauté pork and onions in hot oil for 2 to 3 minutes or until pork is brown and onions are soft. Add soy sauce, ginger and shrimp; cook 4 to 5 minutes longer or until all moisture evaporates. Cool completely.

Unfold 1 puff pastry sheet and, on a lightly floured board, roll to a 12 inch square. Cut into 4 inch squares and put ¼ cup filling in center of each. Fold two opposite *sides* (not corners) of pastry square toward center, overlapping slightly, to form a rectangle. Moisten ends with egg mixture and press with tines of fork to seal. Do not seal top seam. Chill. Repeat with remaining pastry and filling. Place pockets on ungreased cookie sheet and bake in preheated 425° oven for 10 to 12 minutes or until puffed and golden brown. If desired, serve with a Sweet and Sour Sauce.

*Sweet and Sour Sauce

Heat together in a small sauce pan: ½ cup apricot preserves, ¼ cup chutney, 1 tablespoon water and 1½ teaspoons vinegar. Stir constantly until hot and bubbly. Serve warm or cold.

Makes 18 pockets and ¾ cup sauce

Chinese Barbecued Pork
(Char Siu)

½ cup KIKKOMAN Soy Sauce
⅓ cup honey
¼ cup sherry
1 teaspoon red food coloring
¼ teaspoon garlic powder
¼ teaspoon ground ginger
2 pounds boneless pork loin roast (boned, rolled and
   tied)
Mustard-Soy Sauce*
Toasted sesame seed

Blend together soy sauce, honey, sherry, red food coloring, garlic and ginger. Unroll pork roast; cut lengthwise into 3 equal strips. Place in large shallow pan; add marinade and turn over several times to coat thoroughly. Cover and refrigerate 12 to 24 hours, turning over occasionally. Remove pork and lay on rack placed over pan of water. Insert meat thermometer into thickest part of 1 strip. Roast in 325°F oven 30 minutes. Turn strips over and roast about 20 minutes longer, or until meat thermometer registers 165°. Remove from rack and cool at room temperature. At serving time, cut each strip into thin slices. Dip each slice of Chinese Barbecued Pork into Mustard-Soy Sauce, then toasted sesame seed.

Makes about 4 dozen appetizers

*Mustard-Soy Sauce

Blend 2 tablespoons dry mustard with water to make a smooth paste. Thin with KIKKOMAN Soy Sauce to dipping consistency.

Holiday Kabob Classic

8 slices honey loaf or ham (each cut in three equal
   strips)
6 slices pineapple (cut in quarters)
4 tablespoons brown sugar
12 whole maraschino cherries
12 toothpicks

Roll honey loaf strips around each piece of pineapple. Place 2 rollups on a toothpick divided by a maraschino cherry. Sprinkle with brown sugar and broil until glaze develops.

Favorite recipe from **National Hot Dog & Sausage Council**

Shrimp with Sweet-Sour Sauce

2 pounds (21 to 25-count per lb.) raw, unpeeled
    shrimp
1 cup water
⅔ cup cider vinegar
⅔ cup brown sugar, packed
2 tablespoons cornstarch
2 tablespoons **KIKKOMAN Soy Sauce**
½ teaspoon **TABASCO® Pepper Sauce**

Peel shrimp, leaving tails on; devein. Cook in boiling salted water
5 minutes; drain and cool. Wrap and refrigerate. Combine 1 cup
water, vinegar, brown sugar, cornstarch and soy sauce in saucepan. Simmer, stirring constantly, until thickened, about 1 minute.
Cool, cover and store at room temperature. Arrange shrimp in
serving bowl. Add pepper sauce to sweet-sour sauce and bring to
boil, stirring constantly. Pour sauce into serving bowl over candle
warmer and serve with shrimp.

Makes about 2 dozen appetizers and 2 cups sauce

Lipton.

Jolly Shrimp Toast

12 slices white bread
1 envelope **LIPTON® Onion Soup Mix**
2 teaspoons all-purpose flour
2 eggs, slightly beaten
2 pounds uncooked shrimp, cleaned and finely
    chopped
Oil for deep fat frying

Trim crust from bread; cut each slice into 4 triangles. In large
bowl, combine onion soup mix, flour, eggs and shrimp. Spread on
bread and fry, shrimp side down, in hot oil (375°), 2 minutes or
until done; drain.   *Makes 48 appetizers*

FREEZING/REHEATING DIRECTIONS: Tightly wrap appetizers in heavy-duty foil; freeze. To reheat, unwrap and place on
ungreased baking sheet. Bake at 375° 10 minutes or until heated
through. *OR*, place 16 appetizers on paper towel-lined plate;
microwave 3 to 5 minutes or until heated through.

Shrimp Teriyaki

½ cup **KIKKOMAN Soy Sauce**
2 tablespoons sugar
2 tablespoons water
1 tablespoon vegetable oil
1½ teaspoons cornstarch
1 clove garlic, crushed
¼ teaspoon ground ginger *or* 1 teaspoon grated fresh
    ginger root
2 pounds (21 to 25-count per pound) raw shrimp,
    shelled and deveined

Blend soy sauce, sugar, water, oil, cornstarch, garlic and ginger in
saucepan. Simmer, stirring constantly until thickened, about 1
minute. Cool. Coat shrimp in sauce; drain off excess. Place on
rack of broiler pan. Broil 5 inches from heat 3 to 4 minutes on each
side. Remove and cool slightly. Thread each shrimp on short
bamboo skewer; arrange on serving tray. Warm shrimp over charcoal hibachi on buffet table.   *Makes about 4 dozen appetizers*

Sashimi

2 pounds fresh filleted tuna, striped bass or sea bass,
    skinned
3 cups shredded lettuce
Watercress for garnish
2 tablespoons wasabi (Japanese horseradish powder)
    OR dry powdered mustard
Water
½ cup **KIKKOMAN Soy Sauce**

Cut fish into pieces about 1½ inches long, 1 inch wide and ¼-inch
thick. Arrange attractively on bed of shredded lettuce on large
serving plate. Garnish with crisp watercress. Cover plate with
plastic wrap and refrigerate until ready to serve. Meanwhile, blend
wasabi or mustard with small amount of water to form a smooth
paste; cover and let stand 5 minutes. Press together and form into a
cone-shaped ball; place on side of fish on serving plate or divide
equally into serving bowls. Pour about 2 tablespoons soy sauce
into separate dipping dishes, allowing one for each person. Let
each person mix as much wasabi into soy sauce as desired. Dip
cold fish pieces into soy sauce mixture before eating.

Makes 4 to 6 servings

Southern Comfort®
Ginger Shrimp Sauce

½ cup catsup
¼ cup soy sauce
1 teaspoon fresh ginger, finely grated
3 tablespoons brown sugar
3 tablespoons **SOUTHERN COMFORT®**
1 tablespoon cornstarch

Combine catsup, ginger and brown sugar in a small saucepan over
medium heat. In a separate bowl, mix cornstarch with soy sauce
until smooth. Add to mixture in saucepan and stir until boiling.
Continue simmering, uncovered, for 2 minutes. Remove from heat
and stir in **SOUTHERN COMFORT®**.

Irish Mist. *Liqueur*

Bantry Bay Shrimp Toast

1 package (8 oz.) cream cheese, softened
1 can (4½ oz.) shrimp, rinsed and drained
¼ cup mayonnaise
2 tablespoons **IRISH MIST® Liqueur**
1 tablespoon lemon juice
1 tablespoon finely minced parsley
Sliced party rye bread, toasted

In medium bowl, combine all ingredients except toast. Spread on
toast. Broil until lightly browned and puffed. Garnish with shrimp.
Also delicious cold.   *Makes 25*

Mandarin Shrimp

½ lb. **ATALANTA Frozen Shrimp**, raw, shelled, deveined
½ lb. Mandarin orange sections
¼ cup scallions, ½ inch pieces
¼ cup butter, melted

On skewers, alternate shrimp, orange section, scallion and shrimp. Brush with butter and broil 4 minutes on each side.

Yield: 6 Servings

Teriyaki Meat Sticks

½ cup **KIKKOMAN Soy Sauce**
¼ cup chopped green onions and tops
2 tablespoons sugar
1 tablespoon salad oil
1½ teaspoons cornstarch
1 clove garlic, crushed
¼ teaspoon ground ginger (OR 1 teaspoon grated fresh ginger root)
2½ pounds beef sirloin steak, boned and trimmed of fat

Combine soy sauce, green onions, sugar, oil, cornstarch, garlic and ginger in saucepan. Simmer, stirring constantly, until thickened, about 1 minute. Cool, cover and keep at room temperature. Slice meat into ⅛-inch thick strips about 4 inches long and 1 inch wide. Thread bamboo or metal skewers each with 1 strip of meat. Wrap and refrigerate. When ready to serve, brush skewered meat on both sides with sauce. Arrange on serving platter or tray. Let guests cook Meat Sticks on hibachi to desired doneness.

Makes about 5 dozen appetizers

Chinese Fried Walnuts

4 cups water
2 cups walnuts
¼ cup sugar
Soybean oil for frying
Salt

In a 2-quart saucepan, heat water to boiling. Add walnuts; reheat to boiling; boil 1 minute. Drain water from walnuts and rinse under running hot water in colander. Dry walnuts on paper toweling. In large bowl, toss walnuts in sugar. In deep fat fryer or electric skillet, heat oil to 350°F. Fry 1 cup of walnuts at a time for 3-5 minutes, or until golden brown. Stir often to prevent walnuts from sticking together. Remove from oil with slotted spoon or frying basket. Place walnuts in coarse sieve over empty bowl to drain. Sprinkle with salt. Toss lightly. Transfer the walnuts to a waxed paper lined tray to cool. Fry remaining 1 cup of walnuts. When walnuts are cool, store in tightly covered container.

Favorite recipe from **American Soybean Association**

Mushroom Hors D' Oeuvres

⅓ cup rice wine vinegar
1 tablespoon sugar
2 teaspoons **KIKKOMAN Soy Sauce**
Dash monosodium glutamate
1 can (4 oz.) whole mushrooms, drained
Toasted sesame seed

Thoroughly combine vinegar, sugar, soy sauce and monosodium glutamate. Pour over mushrooms and sprinkle with sesame seed. Marinate 30 to 60 minutes. Remove from sauce and serve with wooden picks. OR: Pour sauce over drained whole water chestnuts; marinate overnight in refrigerator.

Makes about 2 dozen appetizers

SweetLite ™

Polynesian Punch

1 small banana, peeled and sliced
1 teaspoon fresh lemon juice
2½ cups pineapple juice, unsweetened
1 cup fresh orange juice
1 teaspoon vanilla extract
1 teaspoon coconut extract
2 teaspoons **SWEETLITE** ™ Fructose
1 cup soda water
Mint sprigs for garnish (optional)

Put the sliced banana in a blender. Add the lemon juice and blend thoroughly. Put all other ingredients except the soda water and mint sprigs in the blender with the banana mixture and blend until frothy. Pour into a large juice container. Add the soda water and mix well.

Makes 8 servings

Each serving contains approximately:
1¼ fruit exchanges
50 calories
0 mg. cholesterol

Soups

Noodle Egg Drop Soup

2 cans (10¾ ounces each) condensed chicken broth
4 cups water
1½ cups (4 ounces) **SKINNER® Fine Egg Noodles**, uncooked
2 eggs, slightly beaten
2 tablespoons chopped parsley
2 tablespoons butter

Bring chicken broth and water to a boil. Gradually add noodles, stirring occasionally; cook 8 minutes. Reduce heat to low; stir in eggs. Simmer 3 minutes longer. Remove from heat; stir in parsley and butter.

4 servings

9

Wyler's®

Egg Drop Soup

6 cups water
2 tablespoons WYLER'S® Chicken-Flavor Instant
  Bouillon *or* 6 Chicken-Flavor Bouillon Cubes
2 tablespoons cornstarch
½ teaspoon monosodium glutamate, optional
1 egg, well beaten
Chopped green onions

In medium saucepan, combine water, bouillon, cornstarch and monosodium glutamate if desired. Cook, stirring constantly until bouillon dissolves. Slowly pour in egg; stir. Heat through. Garnish with onions. Refrigerate leftovers. *Makes about 1½ quarts*

Oriental Soup

½ pound ground pork
1 Tablespoon soy sauce
1 large egg, beaten, divided
1 teaspoon salt, divided
3 teaspoons cornstarch, divided
3 teaspoons dry sherry, divided
½ pound raw shrimp, cut fine
½ teaspoon ginger
8 cups chicken broth
1 package (16 ounces) Frozen STOKELY'S®
  Vegetables Orient®
½ cup thinly sliced bamboo shoots
1½ cups cooked fine noodles

Combine pork, soy sauce, ½ beaten egg, ½ teaspoon salt, 1½ teaspoons cornstarch and 1½ teaspoons sherry. Form into marble-size balls and set aside. Combine shrimp, ginger, remaining egg, salt, cornstarch, and sherry. Shape into marble-size balls and set aside with pork balls. Bring broth to a boil; add vegetables, bamboo shoots, reserved pork and shrimp balls. Cover and simmer over low heat 25 minutes. Stir in noodles, cook until noodles are heated through and adjust seasoning. *4 to 6 servings*

Lea & Perrins
THE ORIGINAL WORCESTERSHIRE

Vegetable Soup Oriental
(Low Calorie)

5 beef bouillon cubes
5 cups boiling water
2 teaspoons LEA & PERRINS Worcestershire Sauce
1 teaspoon soy sauce
1 cup thinly sliced carrots
½ cup sliced scallions or green onions
2½ cups (½ lb.) sliced mushrooms
¼ pound torn spinach

In a medium saucepan combine bouillon cubes, water, LEA & PERRINS, and soy sauce. Bring to boiling point, stirring to dissolve bouillon cubes. Add carrots and scallions. Return to boiling point. Reduce heat and simmer, covered, for 10 minutes. Add mushrooms and spinach. Cover and simmer 5 minutes longer.

Calorie Count: About 36 calories per 1 cup serving

Chinese Vegetable Soup

1 pound boneless pork
1 tablespoon dry sherry
1 tablespoon LA CHOY® Soy Sauce
2 teaspoons minced fresh ginger root
2 teaspoons oil
½ cup sliced fresh mushrooms
½ cup sliced LA CHOY® Bamboo Shoots
½ cup sliced celery
½ cup diced LA CHOY® Water Chestnuts
½ cup diced carrots
8 cups chicken stock
1 pkg. (6 oz.) frozen LA CHOY® Chinese Pea Pods
½ teaspoon salt
2 eggs, beaten

Slice pork across grain into thin strips 2 inches long (slicing is easier if meat is partially frozen). Combine sherry, soy sauce and ginger; mix with pork. Heat oil in wok or large skillet. Add pork and cook over high heat, stirring constantly, until pork is lightly browned. Stir in mushrooms, bamboo shoots, celery, water chestnuts, carrots and broth. Bring to boil; reduce heat and simmer 15 minutes. Add pea pods and salt; cook 5 minutes. Gradually add eggs, stirring until they separate into shreds. Serve immediately. *6 to 8 servings*

DRY SACK
Hot & Sour Soup

4 black dried mushrooms
1 cup water
5 cups chicken broth
1 cup thinly sliced cooked pork
¼ cup DRY SACK® Sherry
1 teaspoon soy sauce
¼ teaspoon ground black pepper
2 tablespoons cornstarch
¼ cup water
1 egg, slightly beaten
1 scallion, minced

Soak mushrooms in one cup water until soft, about 30 minutes. Drain, and thinly slice mushrooms, reserving liquid. Combine chicken broth and reserved mushroom liquid; bring to a boil. Add mushrooms and pork. Simmer, covered, 10 minutes. Stir in DRY SACK® Sherry, soy sauce and pepper. Combine cornstarch and ¼ cup water; add to soup, stirring until mixture thickens slightly. Gradually add egg, stirring only once or twice. Top with scallion. Pour into tureen or individual bowls to serve. *Serves six*

Salads

Cucumber-Orange Salad

1 head **California ICEBERG Lettuce**
1 cup white vinegar
¼ cup sugar
1 tablespoon finely grated orange peel
2 teaspoons salt
½ teaspoon white pepper
½ cup vegetable oil
¼ cup chopped fresh parsley
3 cucumbers (European or hot-house preferred), thinly sliced
3 oranges, thinly sliced
¼ cup toasted sesame seeds

Core, rinse and thoroughly drain lettuce. Refrigerate in plastic bag or plastic crisper. Combine vinegar, sugar, orange peel, salt and pepper in blender. Cover and blend until sugar is dissolved. With blender running, slowly pour in oil. Stir in parsley. Place cucumbers in shallow glass or plastic dish. Pour marinade over. Cover and refrigerate overnight.

To serve: Cut lettuce into bite-size chunks to measure 6 cups. (Refrigerate remainder for future use.) Place chunks in shallow bowl. Drain cucumbers, reserving marinade. Drizzle half of marinade over lettuce; toss gently. Arrange cucumbers over lettuce in alternate rows with orange slices. Drizzle with remaining marinade; sprinkle with sesame seeds.   *Makes 6 to 8 servings*

Favorite recipe from **California Iceberg Lettuce Commission**

Oriental Broccoli and Bean Sprout Salad

2 lb. fresh broccoli
½ lb. fresh mushrooms, cleaned
1 can (16 oz.) **LA CHOY® Bean Sprouts**, rinsed and drained
⅓ cup cider vinegar
⅓ cup salad oil (not olive oil)
2 teaspoons catsup
1 teaspoon salt
Freshly ground black pepper to taste

Cut broccoli florets from stalks. Pare stalks and cut into ¼-inch slices. Cook broccoli stalks in boiling water 1 minute; rinse under cold water and drain. Cook florets 2 minutes in boiling salted water; rinse with cold water and drain. Combine cooked broccoli with mushrooms and bean sprouts. Blend remaining ingredients, pour over vegetables, mixing well. Marinate 1 hour in refrigerator. Serve on crisp lettuce leaves.   *8 servings*

BacOs

Oriental Spinach Salad

Ginger-Soy Dressing*
5 ounces spinach, torn into bite-size pieces
¼ cup sliced water chestnuts
1 green onion (with top), thinly sliced
BAC*OS® Imitation Bacon

Prepare Ginger-Soy Dressing; toss with spinach, water chestnuts and onion. Sprinkle with imitation bacon.   *6 servings*

*Ginger-Soy Dressing

2 tablespoons vegetable oil
1 tablespoon vinegar
2 teaspoons honey
1 teaspoon soy sauce
¼ teaspoon ground ginger

Shake all ingredients in tightly covered container.

Lite Spinach Salad

6 cups spinach leaves
1 can (16 oz.) **DEL MONTE Lite Sliced Peaches**, drained
1 can (15½ oz.) **DEL MONTE Sockeye Red Salmon**
½ cup sliced water chestnuts
6 cherry tomatoes, halved
Gingered Dressing*

Thoroughly clean spinach, drain and tear into bite-size pieces. Combine ingredients and serve with Gingered Dressing.

*Gingered Dressing

½ cup oil
2 Tbsp. vinegar
1 Tbsp. lemon juice
¼ tsp. garlic powder
¼ tsp. ground ginger
Dash salt
Dash pepper

Thoroughly blend all ingredients.   *4 servings*

Pea Pod-Cucumber Salad

2 tablespoons vegetable oil
2 cloves garlic, minced
¼ cup **LA CHOY® Soy Sauce**
¼ cup white vinegar
3 tablespoons sesame oil
2 tablespoons brown sugar
Dash hot pepper sauce
1 package (6 oz.) **LA CHOY® Frozen Chinese Pea Pods**, thawed and drained on paper towels
2 medium cucumbers, peeled, halved, and cut into ¼ inch sticks
1 small celery stalk, julienned

Heat oil in small skillet, add garlic and cook, stirring, until garlic is lightly browned. Add next five ingredients and mix well. Let cool.

One hour before serving, combine vegetables in large serving bowl. Pour dressing over and toss thoroughly. Cover and refrigerate until ready to serve.   *4 servings*

Oriental Sprout Salad

1 package (8 oz.) **OSCAR MAYER Sliced Peppered Loaf**
5 cups (about 12 oz.) Chinese or celery cabbage, thinly sliced
2 cups homegrown sprouts or 1 can (16 oz.) bean sprouts, drained
1 cup sliced fresh mushrooms
1 can (8 oz.) sliced water chestnuts, drained
1 package (7 oz.) frozen snow peas, thawed
2 green onions with tops, chopped
2 tablespoons sesame seeds

Salad Dressing:
½ cup soy sauce
¼ cup vinegar
2 tablespoons oil
2 teaspoons sugar
6 drops bottled hot pepper sauce
Dash dry mustard

Cut stacked sliced meat into ¼-inch strips; separate strips. Place Chinese cabbage into large salad bowl. In medium bowl combine meat, sprouts, mushrooms, water chestnuts, peas and onions; toss. Place on top of cabbage. In large heavy skillet over medium-high heat, toast sesame seeds 2 to 3 minutes stirring often until golden brown. Sprinkle over meat mixture.

In small bowl combine remaining ingredients; blend well. Pass dressing with salad. *Makes 4 (1½ cup) servings*

Note: For fuller flavor marinate mushrooms 1 hour in salad dressing.

San Giorgio®

Rickshaw Salad

3 cups (12-ounces) **SAN GIORGIO® Fusilli**, uncooked
¾ cup salad dressing or mayonnaise
¼ cup soy sauce
1 teaspoon hot mustard
1 teaspoon salt
½ teaspoon garlic powder
¼ teaspoon pepper
1½ cups (16-ounce can) bean sprouts, drained
1 cup frozen peas, thawed
½ cup sliced celery
½ cup chopped green pepper
½ cup chopped onion
1 cup (8-ounce can) water chestnuts, drained and sliced
⅔ cup (4-ounce can) sliced mushrooms, drained

Cook Fusilli according to package directions; drain well. Cool. (Rinse with cold water to cool quickly; drain well.)

Combine salad dressing or mayonnaise, soy sauce, hot mustard, salt, garlic powder and pepper in small bowl; blend well. Combine cooled Fusilli, bean sprouts, peas, celery, green pepper, onion, water chestnuts and sliced mushrooms in large bowl. Pour mayonnaise mixture over pasta and vegetables; toss lightly until ingredients are evenly coated. Chill. *8 to 10 servings*

Oriental Salad

1 package (16 ounces) **Frozen STOKELY'S® Vegetables Japanese**
2 cups sliced celery
½ cup sliced water chestnuts
¼ cup sliced green onions
¼ cup oil
4 teaspoons soy sauce
1 teaspoon lemon juice
½ teaspoon salt
½ teaspoon ginger
⅛ teaspoon pepper
2 Tablespoons **STOKELY'S FINEST® Sliced Pimientos**

Cook vegetables half the required time on package directions. Drain. In large bowl, combine cooked vegetables, celery, water chestnuts and green onions. Combine remaining ingredients, except pimiento. Pour over vegetable mixture; toss well. Cover and chill at least one hour before serving. Garnish with pimiento. *8 servings*

Calories: Only 93 calories per serving

Creamy Mandarin Rice Salad

3 cups cool cooked **DORE® Rice**
1 can (16 ounces) Mandarin orange segments, drained
1½ cups thinly sliced celery
½ cup diced green pepper
¾ cup sour cream
1 tablespoon lemon juice
1 teaspoon *each* seasoned salt and seasoned pepper

Blend all ingredients thoroughly. Chill. Serve on salad greens and sprinkle with sliced almonds, if desired. *Makes 6 servings*

Classic Rice Salad

3 cups cool cooked rice
½ cup *each* finely chopped onions and sweet pickles
1 teaspoon salt
¼ teaspoon pepper
1 cup mayonnaise
1 teaspoon prepared mustard
¼ cup diced pimientos
4 hard-cooked eggs, chopped

Blend all ingredients thoroughly. Chill. Serve on lettuce leaves, if desired. *Makes 6 generous servings*

Favorite recipe from **Rice Council of America**

Strawberry Rice Salad

⅓ cup vegetable oil
⅓ cup sherry
¼ cup white vinegar
2 tablespoons soy sauce
1½ tablespoons sugar
1 large clove garlic, pressed
½ teaspoon ginger
¼ teaspoon pepper
3 cups cooked rice
1 can (8 ounces) water chestnuts, drained and diced
¼ cup sliced green onions
2 tablespoons chopped parsley
1 pint basket fresh California strawberries, stemmed and halved
Lettuce leaves

In large bowl whisk together oil, sherry, vinegar, soy sauce, sugar, garlic, ginger and pepper. Add rice, water chestnuts, onions and parsley. Toss to combine thoroughly. Cover and chill at least 4 hours or overnight. Just before serving mix in berries. Spoon into lettuce-lined bowl. Sprinkle with additional chopped parsley, if desired.   *Makes 6 servings*

Favorite recipe from **California Strawberry Advisory Board**

Chop Suey Salad

1 can (13½ or 14½ ounces) chicken broth
1 cup **UNCLE BEN'S® CONVERTED® Brand Rice**
1½ teaspoons salt
½ cup vegetable oil
2 tablespoons soy sauce
2 tablespoons toasted sesame seeds (optional)
2 cups diced cooked chicken, turkey or pork
1 can (14 ounces) chop suey vegetables, drained
1 jar (4½ ounces) sliced mushrooms, drained
4 green onions with tops, sliced
1 jar (2 ounces) diced pimiento, drained

Add enough water to broth to make 2½ cups liquid. Bring to a boil. Stir in rice and 1 teaspoon of salt. Cover and simmer 20 minutes. Remove from heat. Let stand covered until all liquid is absorbed, about 5 minutes. Transfer rice to large bowl. Combine oil, soy sauce, remaining ½ teaspoon salt and sesame seeds, if desired, mixing well. Stir into rice. Cover and refrigerate 1 hour. Stir in remaining ingredients. Cover and chill at least 3 hours.
Makes 6 main dish servings

Oriental Surprise

¾ pound cooked, peeled, deveined shrimp, fresh or frozen
1 package (10 ounces) frozen peas, cooked and drained
1 cup finely chopped celery
½ cup mayonnaise
1 tablespoon lemon juice
½ teaspoon curry powder
⅛ teaspoon garlic salt
⅛ teaspoon pepper
1 can (3 ounces) chow mein noodles
½ cup salted cashew nuts
Salad greens

Thaw shrimp if frozen. Cut large shrimp in half. Combine first 8 ingredients in large bowl and mix well; chill. Add noodles and nuts; toss lightly. Serve on salad greens.   *Makes 4 servings*

Favorite recipe from **Gulf and South Atlantic Fisheries Development Foundation, Inc.**

Mandarin Crab Salad

1 (6 oz.) pkg. **WAKEFIELD® Crabmeat**
1 (11 oz.) can mandarin oranges, drained
2 grapefruits, peeled and sectioned
1 cup thinly sliced celery
½ cup pecan pieces
1 (3 oz.) can chow mein noodles
Salad greens

Ginger Dressing:

½ cup mayonnaise
1½ teaspoons lemon juice
¼ teaspoon powdered ginger

Thaw and drain crabmeat. Combine with oranges, grapefruit, celery and nuts. Line four salad plates with crisp salad greens; place a mound of noodles in center of each plate and top with crab and fruit mixture. Serve with ginger dressing.

Tuna Helper®

Oriental Tuna Salad

1 package **BETTY CROCKER® TUNA HELPER® Mix for Creamy Noodles 'n Tuna**
3 cups hot water
1 cup diagonally sliced celery
1 can (8 ounces) water chestnuts, drained and sliced
1 can (6½ ounces) tuna, drained
1 package (6 ounces) frozen Chinese pea pods, thawed and drained
1 jar (2 ounces) sliced pimientos, drained
¼ cup vegetable oil
3 tablespoons vinegar
1 tablespoon soy sauce
2 teaspoons sugar
½ teaspoon pepper
¼ to ½ teaspoon ground ginger

Heat Noodles, Sauce Mix and water to boiling in 10-inch skillet, stirring constantly. Reduce heat; cover and simmer, stirring occasionally, 10 minutes. Simmer uncovered 5 minutes longer; cool 5 minutes. Mix celery, water chestnuts, tuna, pea pods and pimientos in large bowl. Mix remaining ingredients; toss with tuna mixture. Stir in noodle mixture. Serve immediately, or if desired, cover and refrigerate until chilled, at least 3 hours.

4 or 5 servings

HIGH ALTITUDE DIRECTIONS (3500 to 6500 feet): Increase hot water to 3¼ cups and first simmer time to 15 minutes.

Shrimp Salad Polynesian

1 lb. **ATALANTA Frozen Shrimp**, cooked, peeled, deveined
1 large red apple, cored and cubed
1½ cups pineapple chunks
½ lb. grapes, green, seedless
1 cup yogurt, plain
1 Tbsp. curry powder
3 Tbsp. lemon juice
Lettuce leaves, Bibb or Romaine, as needed

Combine yogurt, curry powder and lemon juice. Mix well. Combine shrimp, cubed apple, pineapple chunks and grapes. Toss gently with yogurt dressing. Serve on lettuce leaves.

Yield: 4 servings

San Giorgio®

Chinese Chicken Salad

⅓ cup soy sauce
1½ tablespoons vegetable or sesame oil
1 tablespoon prepared mustard
2 cups cooked chicken, cut into thin strips
1¼ cups (8 ounces) **SAN GIORGIO® Orzo**, uncooked
8-ounce package (about 2 cups) frozen snow peas
½ cup sliced green onion
1 cup (8-ounce can) sliced water chestnuts, drained
Tomato rose, optional

Blend soy sauce, oil and mustard in medium bowl; add chicken and toss lightly until well coated. Allow to stand about 1 hour to blend flavors. Cook Orzo according to package directions; drain well. Cool. (Rinse with cold water to cool quickly; drain well.)

Cook snow peas according to package directions; drain well. Cool. Gently combine chicken mixture, cooled Orzo, snow peas, green onion and water chestnuts until blended. Chill. Garnish with a tomato rose, if desired. Serve.   *About 4 servings*

Chicken Chow Mein Salad

1½ cups cubed cooked chicken
1 can (16 oz.) **VEG-ALL® Mixed Vegetables**, drained and chilled
6 hard-cooked eggs, sliced
1 cup diced celery
¼ cup coarsely chopped green pepper
¼ cup chopped pimiento
¾ cup real mayonnaise
2 Tbsp. minced onion
1 tsp. fresh lemon juice or to taste
½ tsp. salt or to taste
¼ tsp. freshly ground pepper
1 (5 oz.) can chow mein noodles

Garnish:
Green pepper strips
Pimiento strips

Combine chicken, **VEG-ALL®**, eggs, celery, green pepper, and pimiento; toss gently just to mix. Combine mayonnaise, onion, lemon juice, salt and pepper; blend into chicken mixture. Refriger-

ate. To serve, mound chicken salad in center of serving platter and surround with chow mein noodles. Garnish with additional strips of green pepper and pimiento.   *Serves 4 to 6*

Coriander Chicken Salad

1 head **California ICEBERG Lettuce**
1 roasting chicken, 4½ to 5 pounds, cut up
Oil for frying
2 tablespoons sesame seed
1 bunch green onion tops
1 bunch coriander (Chinese parsley)
1 tablespoon hot mustard
½ teaspoon monosodium glutamate (optional)
¼ teaspoon salt
¼ teaspoon sugar

Core, rinse and thoroughly drain lettuce; refrigerate in plastic bag or plastic crisper. Deep fry chicken; cool. Strip meat from bones and shred finely. Toast sesame seed in ungreased skillet. Finely shred onion tops. Remove stems from coriander. Mix chicken with hot mustard and add sesame seed, reserving some for garnish. Add monosodium glutamate, salt, sugar, onion and coriander; toss to mix. Remove outer lettuce leaves from head and line serving dish. Shred remaining lettuce; by halving head lengthwise, then place cut-sides down and cut crosswise. Place shredded lettuce atop leaves on serving dish. Heap chicken mixture on lettuce. Garnish with reserved sesame seed and, if desired, additional coriander.

Makes 4 servings

Favorite recipe from **California Iceberg Lettuce Commission**

Meat

Beef

Teriyaki Beef Kabobs

1 packet **BUTTER BUDS®**, made into liquid
2 tablespoons dry sherry
1 tablespoon lemon juice
1 tablespoon soy sauce
2 teaspoons sugar
1 clove garlic, minced
¼ teaspoon ginger
1 pound top round beef, cut into 1½-inch chunks
1 medium-size green pepper, seeded and cut into 1-inch chunks
1 can (8 ounces) juice-packed pineapple chunks, drained
1 medium-size onion, cut into 1-inch chunks

In medium-size bowl, combine **BUTTER BUDS®**, sherry, lemon juice, soy sauce, sugar, garlic, and ginger. Add beef and stir to coat thoroughly. Cover and refrigerate 2 to 3 hours, stirring occasionally.

Remove beef cubes and reserve marinade. Thread beef, green pepper, pineapple, and onion alternately on four 10-inch wood or

metal skewers. Cook 10 to 15 minutes on preheated barbecue grill, turning once during cooking and basting several times with marinade.
4 servings

PER SERVING (1 skewer): Calories: 285   Protein: 25gm
Carbohydrate: 15gm   Fat: 10gm   Sodium: 615mg

Teriyaki Comfort®

1 cup water
½ cup soy sauce
½ cup **SOUTHERN COMFORT®**
Large clove of garlic (crushed)
¼ cup sugar
½ teaspoon powdered ginger
3 tablespoons oil

Cut 2 lb. of boneless beef (sirloin, round, tenderloin or chuck) into thin strips, 1½ x 4 inches. Marinate from 6 to 8 hours (longer if chuck is used) and then string on skewers. The meat should be cooked quickly on both sides over a hot charcoal fire.

sunlite®

Flank Steak Teriyaki

½ cup soy sauce
⅓ cup **SUNLITE® Oil**
¼ cup honey
2 Tablespoons red wine vinegar
1 clove garlic, minced
1 teaspoon ground ginger
2 to 3 lb. flank steak

In a small bowl or jar with tight fitting lid, combine *all* ingredients *except* steak; mix well. Score flank steak. Place in glass baking dish(es). Pour teriyaki marinade over meat. Refrigerate 3 to 8 hours; turn once. Broil steak about 5 minutes per side or to desired doneness, basting with marinade. To serve slice thinly across grain.
Makes 6 to 8 servings

Teriyaki Shish Kabobs

1 (3-pound) round steak (about 1½-inches thick), cut into cubes
1 (15¼-ounce) can pineapple chunks, drained
8 ounces (about 2 cups) small whole fresh mushrooms, cleaned
3 medium onions, quartered and separated into bite-size pieces
2 medium green peppers, cut into bite-size pieces
1 pint cherry tomatoes
Teriyaki Marinade*
Hot cooked rice

Prepare vegetables and meat; place all but tomatoes in large shallow baking dish. Pour Teriyaki Marinade on top. Marinate overnight; stir occasionally. Skewer marinated ingredients with tomatoes. Grill or broil to desired doneness; brush with marinade during cooking. Serve over rice. Refrigerate leftovers.
Makes 8 servings
(Continued)

*Teriyaki Marinade

1 cup firmly-packed **COLONIAL® Light Golden Brown Sugar**
⅔ cup catsup
⅔ cup vinegar
½ cup soy sauce
½ cup vegetable oil
5 to 6 cloves garlic, finely chopped
2 teaspoons ground ginger

In medium bowl, combine ingredients; mix well.

Tip: Teriyaki Marinade is also delicious when used to marinate pork chops or chicken.

Teriyaki Meat Marinade

½ cup soy sauce
¼ cup **DOMINO® Liquid Brown Sugar**
¼ cup dry sherry
1 teaspoon ground ginger
1½ lb. cubed beef, chicken, pork, or whole flank steak

Combine soy sauce, **DOMINO® Liquid Brown Sugar**, dry sherry, and ground ginger. Pour over meat. Refrigerate at least 4 hours. Baste meat with remaining sauce while barbecuing or broiling.

Cantonese Flank Steak

½ pound flank steak
2 Tablespoons cornstarch
1 teaspoon sugar
½ teaspoon ginger
½ cup dry sherry
2 Tablespoons soy sauce
⅓ cup water
1 teaspoon plus 1 Tablespoon vegetable oil, divided
1 package (14 ounces) **Frozen STOKELY'S® Cantonese Style Stir Fry Vegetables**

Cut flank steak across the grain into paper-thin strips.* Place in glass dish. Blend cornstarch, sugar, ginger, sherry, soy sauce, and water to make marinade. Pour marinade over meat. Refrigerate, covered, 2½ hours. Remove meat from marinade and drain, reserving marinade. Heat 9- or 10-inch skillet or wok over high heat (a drop of water will sizzle). Pour 1 teaspoon oil in wide, circular motion inside rim of pan. Tilt pan to coat surface. Add half the meat and stir-fry about 3 minutes. Remove to warm serving dish. Cook remaining meat about 3 minutes and remove to serving dish. Remove seasoning packet from vegetables and reserve. When skillet is again very hot, spread frozen vegetables evenly in pan. Pour 1 Tablespoon oil in pan in circular motion and stir into vegetables quickly, coating each piece. Sprinkle reserved seasoning packet over vegetables and add 2 Tablespoons water and reserved marinade in circular motion. Cook and stir about 30 seconds until vegetables and seasonings are blended. Cover and cook 1 minute, return meat to skillet, stir, and cook 1 minute more. Serve immediately.
4 servings

*Note: For easier slicing, partially freeze flank steak.

KUBLA KHAN

Fried Beef with Chinese Peapods

½ lb. beef, sliced and cut into bite size pieces
1 tablespoon wine
3 tablespoons soy sauce
2 teaspoons cornstarch
6 tablespoons oil
1 package **KUBLA KHAN Chinese Peapods** (thawed)
1 clove garlic, crushed
½ teaspoon sugar
½ teaspoon monosodium glutamate

Dredge beef with 1 tablespoon wine, 1 tablespoon soy sauce, and 2 teaspoons cornstarch. Heat 4 tablespoons oil and fry beef. When color changes, remove to a plate. Heat 2 tablespoons oil and fry (2 minutes) Chinese Peapods. Add beef, garlic, 2 tablespoons soy sauce, sugar and monosodium glutamate. Mix well and serve hot.

Serves 2

Mazola®

Stir-Fry Beef and Green Beans

2 tablespoons soy sauce
2 tablespoons dry sherry
1 clove garlic, crushed
1 teaspoon sugar
½ teaspoon ground ginger
1 pound beef, thinly sliced diagonally (flank or round steak)
⅓ cup **MAZOLA® Corn Oil**, divided
1 pound green beans, diagonally sliced in ¾-inch pieces
1 cup thinly sliced onion
½ teaspoon salt
¼ teaspoon dried, crushed red pepper
2 tablespoons **ARGO®/KINGSFORD'S® Corn Starch**
1½ cups beef broth

In medium bowl stir together soy sauce, sherry, garlic, sugar and ginger. Add beef and marinate at least 1 hour. In large skillet or wok heat 3 tablespoons of the corn oil over medium high heat. Add green beans, onions and salt and stir fry 4 minutes or until tender-crisp. Remove. Add remaining corn oil and heat over medium-high heat. Add beef, red pepper; stir fry 2 minutes or until browned. Return beans to pan. Stir beef broth into corn starch until smooth. Add to skillet. Stirring constantly, bring to boil over medium heat and boil 1 minute. *Makes 4 to 6 servings*

VARIATIONS:

Beef and Cauliflower

Follow basic recipe. Substitute 1 small head cauliflower for green beans. Break cauliflower into flowerettes, then slice. Stir in 1 jar (2 oz) sliced pimiento, drained.

(Continued)

Beef and Mushrooms

Follow basic recipe. Substitute 1 pound mushrooms, sliced, and 1 cup thinly sliced green pepper for green beans. Reduce stir-fry time to 2 minutes.

Beef and Chinese Vegetables

Follow basic recipe. Substitute 1 cup diagonally sliced celery, 1 cup sliced mushrooms, 1 can (8 oz) water chestnuts, drained, sliced and 1 can (8½ oz) sliced bamboo shoots, drained for green beans. Reduce stir-fry time to 3 minutes.

Note: 1 pound boneless chicken breasts, thinly sliced, may be substituted for beef.

Aromatic Sukiyaki

2½ lb. well marbled sirloin
2 cups thinly sliced carrots
2 cups thinly sliced celery
1 cup finely chopped onions
1 can (8 oz.) bamboo shoots, drained and sliced
1 can (8½ oz.) water chestnuts, drained and sliced
1 tablespoon sugar
¼ cup soy sauce
1 cup beef broth
1 tablespoon **ANGOSTURA® Aromatic Bitters**

Cut fat from outer edge of sirloin and reserve. To slice meat thinly, freeze until hard, then cut into paper thin strips about 1½ inches wide. Arrange meat and all vegetables on a tray. Combine all remaining ingredients and keep in a bowl. Dice reserved fat and fry in a large skillet until crisp. Remove crisp pieces and add meat to hot fat. Cook meat quickly over very high heat. Add vegetables and cook while stirring. Add liquid mixture. Cover and let steam for 5 minutes or until vegetables are tender crisp.

Yield: 6 servings

Beef Sukiyaki in Wok
(Low Calorie)

1 medium onion, sliced
1 pound beef sirloin, cut in thin strips
1 teaspoon salt
¼ teaspoon pepper
1 tablespoon vinegar
½ pound fresh mushrooms, sliced
½ cup sliced celery
½ cup green pepper strips
1 (12 oz.) can **DIET SHASTA® Lemon-Lime**
3 tablespoons soy sauce
1 beef bouillon cube, crumbled
1 (16 oz.) can bean sprouts, drained
1 (4⅔ oz.) can bamboo shoots, drained
1 (8 oz.) can water chestnuts, drained and sliced

Sauté onion in large skillet until softened. Add beef strips. Cook and stir over high heat until lightly browned. Sprinkle with salt, pepper and vinegar. Add mushrooms, celery and green pepper. Cook 5 minutes. Add all remaining ingredients and simmer 5 minutes. *Serves 5 or 6*

Calories: 151 per serving

Sukiyaki-Style Beef and Vegetables

1 Golden Delicious apple
1 cup beef bouillon
2 tablespoons soy sauce
1 cup sliced broccoli
1 medium onion, sliced
½ pound lean beef, thinly sliced
1 cup sliced Chinese cabbage or thinly sliced head cabbage
1 cup sliced mushrooms

Core and slice apple. Combine beef bouillon and soy sauce in skillet; bring to boil, add broccoli and onions; simmer until crisp-tender. Add remaining ingredients; simmer until barely cooked. Serve with rice. *Makes 4 servings*

Calories: 189 calories each
Favorite recipe from **The Apple Growers of Washington State**

Pepper Steak

1 pound round steak (cut in thin strips)
1 cup sliced green pepper
1 cup sliced onion
½ cup coarsely chopped celery
1 cup sliced mushrooms
2 Tbsp. butter or margarine
1 tsp. salt
2 Tbsp. soy sauce
1 Tbsp. corn starch
1 cup water
1-1½ tsp. **BALTIMORE SPICE OLD BAY Seasoning**

In skillet, brown round steak slightly in butter or margarine. Add vegetables, salt and **BALTIMORE SPICE OLD BAY Seasoning**. Stir fry about 5 minutes. Mix corn starch with water and soy sauce. Pour over vegetables. Heat and stir until sauce is thick and slightly transparent. Serve over rice. *6 servings*

Pepper Beef

1 pound flank steak, partially frozen and cut diagonally into strips
2 tablespoons vegetable oil
3 cups water
1 tablespoon Beef-flavor instant bouillon or 3 beef-flavor bouillon cubes
3 tablespoons cornstarch
3 tablespoons soy sauce
1 cup sliced celery
1 medium green pepper, cut into 1-inch pieces
1 firm medium tomato, cut into eighths
½ (1-pound) package **CREAMETTE® Egg Noodles**, cooked as package directs and drained

In large skillet, cook beef in oil over medium high heat until browned and liquid is absorbed. Add water and bouillon. Stir together cornstarch and soy sauce. Add to skillet; cook, stirring constantly, until thickened and clear. Reduce heat to medium; add celery and green pepper. Cook 5 to 8 minutes. Add tomato; cook 5 minutes longer. Serve over hot cooked noodles with additional soy sauce if desired. Refrigerate leftovers. *Makes 6 servings*

Chinese Pepper Steak

1 to 1½ lb. boneless top round or sirloin steak
2 tablespoons oil
1 clove garlic, minced
1 teaspoon salt
1 cup canned undiluted beef broth (bouillon)
1 cup thinly sliced green pepper strips
1 cup thinly sliced celery
¼ cup thinly sliced onions
½ cup **COCA-COLA®**
2 medium, ripe tomatoes
2½ tablespoons corn starch
¼ cup **COCA-COLA®**
1 tablespoon soy sauce
Hot cooked rice

Trim all fat from meat and cut into pencil-thin strips. In deep skillet or Dutch oven, heat oil, garlic and salt. Add meat and brown over high heat about 10 minutes, stirring occasionally with a fork. Add beef broth, cover and simmer 15 to 20 minutes, or until meat is fork-tender. Stir in green pepper, celery, onions and ½ cup **COCA-COLA®**. Cover; simmer 5 minutes. Do not over-cook; vegetables should be tender-crisp. Peel tomatoes, cut into wedges, gently stir into meat. Blend corn starch with the ¼ cup **COCA-COLA®** and soy sauce. Stir into meat and cook until thickened, about 1 minute, stirring lightly with fork. Serve over hot rice. *Makes 6 (¾ cup) servings*

Holland House®

Sara's Pepper Steak

2 pounds thickly sliced filet steak
¼ cup flour
1 cup butter
2 green peppers, sliced
2 onions, sliced
2 cloves garlic, minced
½ pound mushrooms, sliced
3 small tomatoes, quartered
1½ cups beef bouillon
2 tablespoons cornstarch
¾ cup **HOLLAND HOUSE® Red Cooking Wine**
2 tablespoons soy sauce
Salt and pepper to taste

Dip steak in flour. In large skillet, sauté in half the butter for 2 minutes. Remove meat. Add remaining butter and sauté peppers, onions, garlic and mushrooms 5 minutes. Add tomatoes and bouillon. Bring to a boil, reduce heat, simmer 10 minutes. Mix cornstarch, **HOLLAND HOUSE® Red Cooking Wine** and soy sauce. Add to skillet. Cook, stirring, until thickened. Add salt and pepper to taste. Add meat. Simmer 5 minutes. Serve with Chinese noodles or rice. *Serves 4-6*

Note: To use less tender cuts of meat such as round or flank steak, slice meat paper thin. Brown as above, without flour, but return to skillet with bouillon.

Lipton.

Delish-Kabobs

1 envelope **LIPTON® Onion Soup Mix**
1 cup dry red wine
¼ cup oil
1 tablespoon soy sauce
1 clove garlic, finely chopped
2-pound boneless round steak, cut into 2-inch cubes
12 mushroom caps
½ pint cherry tomatoes
2 small green peppers, cut into chunks

In large shallow baking dish, combine **LIPTON® Onion Soup Mix,** wine, oil, soy sauce and garlic; add beef. Cover and marinate in refrigerator, turning occasionally, 4 hours or overnight.

On skewers, alternately thread beef, mushrooms, tomatoes and green peppers. Grill or broil, turning and basting frequently with remaining marinade, until done. *About 6 servings*

Ginger Beef with Raisin Sauce

1½ pounds tender beef steak
2 tablespoons flour
1½ teaspoons ginger
1 teaspoon paprika
1 teaspoon seasoned salt
3 tablespoons oil
⅓ cup California raisins
2 tablespoons butter or margarine
1 teaspoon soy sauce
3 tablespoons catsup
½ cup bouillon or water

Cut steak in thin strips. Dredge in flour mixed with ginger, paprika and salt. Brown in hot oil; remove from pan and keep hot. Add remaining ingredients to pan, stirring well. Simmer 2 to 3 minutes. Add steak and heat. Serve with rice. *Serves 4 to 6*

Favorite recipe from **California Raisin Advisory Board**

ARGO®/ KINGSFORD'S®

Marinated Beef Strips

½ cup **KARO® Dark** or **Light Corn Syrup**
¼ cup soy sauce
2 tablespoons vinegar
1 tablespoon chopped candied ginger OR ¼ teaspoon ground ginger
1 clove garlic, finely minced
2 pounds round steak, cut across the grain into thin strips
2 teaspoons **ARGO®/KINGSFORD'S® Corn Starch**
2 tablespoons water
Hot cooked rice

Combine corn syrup, soy sauce, vinegar, ginger and garlic. Pour over meat in shallow bowl. Let marinate in refrigerator *at least* 3

hours, turning occasionally. Pour all into skillet. Bring to boil. Cover; simmer until meat is tender and done, about 30 minutes. Blend corn starch and water. Stir into sauce. Boil 1 minute, stirring constantly. Serve over rice. *Makes 8 servings*

SUE BEE HONEY

Dressed-Up Steak

3 pounds round steak
1 teaspoon salt
2 tablespoons salad oil or drippings
1 large onion, sliced
1 medium green pepper, diced
1½ cups chopped celery
1 can (1 lb. 4½ oz.) pineapple chunks
1 fresh tomato, cubed
1 tablespoon corn starch
¼ cup **SUE BEE® Honey**
1 tablespoon soy sauce or Worcestershire sauce

Cut meat in cubes; season with salt. Brown in oil. Remove meat and set aside. In the same skillet, sauté the onion, green pepper, and celery for about five minutes. Drain pineapple; reserve half-cup of juice. Add pineapple chunks and tomatoes to sautéed vegetables. Moisten corn starch with pineapple juice, add honey and soy sauce or Worcestershire. Blend into vegetables, add meat. Cover and cook at 325° (slow) two hours or until tender, stirring occasionally to blend and prevent sticking. *Makes six servings*

Lea & Perrins
THE ORIGINAL WORCESTERSHIRE

Polynesian Pot Roast

1 can (8½ oz.) pineapple tidbits
2 tablespoons brown sugar
½ teaspoon ground ginger
½ cup chopped onion
⅓ cup cider vinegar
3 tablespoons soy sauce
2 tablespoons oil
1 tablespoon **LEA & PERRINS Worcestershire Sauce**
5-pound beef chuck arm pot roast
1 can (10½ oz.) condensed beef broth
1½ teaspoons salt
3 cups peeled sweet potato chunks
2 tablespoons cornstarch
2 tablespoons cold water

Combine pineapple, brown sugar, ginger, onion, vinegar, soy sauce, oil and **LEA & PERRINS**. Place beef in a snug-fitting bowl or doubled plastic bag. Pour pineapple mixture over meat. Cover or fasten. Refrigerate for 12 hours, mixing or turning once. Place beef and the pineapple marinade in a large saucepot or Dutch oven. Add broth and salt. Bring to boiling point. Reduce heat and simmer, covered, for 1½ hours. Add sweet potatoes. Simmer, covered, for ½ hour. Remove beef to a warm platter. Blend cornstarch with water. Stir into liquid in saucepot. Cook and stir until sauce thickens. Serve hot with the pot roast.

Cantonese Beef Stew

1 lb. round steak, cut in 2 inch strips
1 clove garlic, minced
1 Tbsp. cooking oil
2 cups stock or 1 bouillon cube mixed with
    2 cups water
1 Tbsp. **CHINA BEAUTY® Soy Sauce**
½ tsp. sugar
¼ tsp. salt
¼ tsp. thyme or ginger
1 cup green onions, cut in 1 inch pieces
1 pkg. frozen green peas
1 cup sliced celery
1 small can **CHINA BEAUTY® Water Chestnuts**,
    drained and sliced
1 can **CHINA BEAUTY® Bean Sprouts**, drained
2 diced tomatoes
1 Tbsp. cornstarch

Sauté beef and garlic in oil until lightly browned. Add 1 cup of stock, and the seasonings. Cover and cook slowly until meat is tender, about 45 minutes. Add onions, peas and celery and cook for 5 minutes more, then add water chestnuts, bean sprouts and tomatoes; Heat through. Combine remaining cup of stock with cornstarch, mix with stew and simmer until sauce is clear and thickened; add more soy sauce if desired. Serve with chow mein noodles or rice.

4-5 servings

GRANDMA'S® MOLASSES

Sweet 'n Sour Stew

2 pounds beef chuck, cut into 1½-inch cubes
3 tablespoons flour
1 tablespoon salad oil
1 can (1 pound) tomatoes
2 medium onions, sliced
1 teaspoon celery salt
1 teaspoon salt
¼ teaspoon pepper
⅓ cup vinegar
⅓ cup **GRANDMA'S® Unsulphured Molasses**
1 cup water
3 large or 4 medium carrots, pared and cut into 1-inch
    pieces
½ cup raisins
½ teaspoon ginger

Coat beef with the flour. Brown in oil in heavy saucepan; add tomatoes, onions, celery salt, salt and pepper. Mix vinegar, molasses and water; add to meat. Cover and simmer until meat is almost tender, about 2 hours. Add carrots, raisins and ginger. Cook until carrots and meat are tender, 30 to 40 minutes. Serve over hot cooked rice.
Yield: 6 servings

Shoyu-Pickled Beef

½ cup **KIKKOMAN Soy Sauce**
½ cup mirin (sweet rice wine) or sherry
2 cloves garlic, crushed
1 pound boneless tender beef, thinly sliced

Combine soy sauce, mirin and garlic. Arrange part of beef slices in single layer in shallow pan. Pour part of soy sauce mixture over beef. Repeat procedure with remaining beef and sauce. Marinate in refrigerator 12 to 24 hours. Remove from marinade and broil to desired degree of doneness. *Makes 2 to 4 servings*

Spicy Barbecue Sauce

½ cup **SUE BEE® Honey**
¼ cup soy sauce
¼ cup lemon juice
2 tablespoons steak sauce (bottled)
1 teaspoon dry mustard
1 teaspoon ground ginger
⅛ teaspoon ground cloves

Combine ingredients in small saucepan. Bring to a boil and remove from heat. *Makes about 1 cup*

Ground Beef

Sweet & Sour Meat Balls

1½ lb. chopped meat
1 onion
1 egg
1 can **ROKEACH Tomato Mushroom Sauce**
2 Tbsp. lemon juice
3 Tbsp. sugar
Salt and pepper to taste

Pour the can of **ROKEACH Tomato Mushroom Sauce** and one can of water in a large saucepan with cover. Bring to a boil. Add lemon juice and sugar. Mix meat with egg, onion, salt and pepper. Make small balls of mixture and add to sauce. Cook for about ¾ hour until done. Serve with cooked broad noodles.
Serves 4 people

FISHER®

Fisher'®s Sweet 'n Sour Meatballs

Meat Balls:
1 pound ground beef
1 egg
⅛ teaspoon pepper
⅛ teaspoon garlic powder
1 teaspoon instant minced onion
2 tablespoons tomato paste
¾ cup dry bread crumbs
¼ cup **FISHER'®S Salted, Roasted Sunflower Nuts**
Vegetable oil for frying

Sauce:
1 bottle (1 lb.) barbecue sauce
1 jar (10 oz.) grape jelly
Hot cooked rice

Combine ingredients for meat balls; shape into 20 balls. Brown in hot oil in skillet; drain off fat. Add barbecue sauce and jelly; cover and simmer 1 hour. Serve atop bed of steaming hot rice (regular or wild). *Makes 5 servings*

RAGÚ
Sweet 'n Sour Meatballs

½ pound ground beef
½ pound ground pork
½ cup seasoned breadcrumbs
1 egg
2 tablespoons milk
½ teaspoon garlic powder
½ teaspoon salt
¼ teaspoon pepper
2 tablespoons vegetable oil
1 jar (15½ oz.) RAGÚ´ Spaghetti Sauce, any flavor
½ cup finely chopped onion
¼ cup vinegar
2 tablespoons Worcestershire sauce
2 tablespoons brown sugar
2 teaspoons prepared mustard
3 cups cooked rice

In a large bowl, combine first 8 ingredients; mix thoroughly. Shape into 1 inch meatballs. In a large skillet, brown meatballs in hot oil; drain fat. Add next 6 ingredients; stir gently. Simmer, partially covered, 30 minutes or until meatballs are done. Serve over rice.

Serves 4

Chinese Sweet 'n Sour Beef

1 lb. lean ground beef
3 tablespoons A.1. Steak Sauce
1 egg, beaten
½ cup soft bread crumbs
1 medium clove garlic, crushed
1 teaspoon salt
1 tablespoon oil
1 can (8 oz.) pineapple chunks, in unsweetened juice, undrained
1 cup *each* sliced carrots and sliced celery
¼ teaspoon ground ginger
1 tablespoon cider vinegar
2 tablespoons *each* A.1. Steak Sauce and soy sauce
¾ cup beef broth
1 tablespoon *each* cornstarch and water
1 large green pepper, cut in strips
1 cup rice, cooked

Lightly mix beef, 3 tablespoons A.1., egg, bread crumbs, garlic, and salt. Form into 24 meatballs. In large skillet, brown meatballs well in oil. Drain. Add remaining ingredients except cornstarch, water and green pepper. Simmer, covered, 5 minutes. Combine cornstarch and water. Stir into mixture. Add green pepper. Simmer, uncovered 5 minutes. Serve on bed of rice. *Serves 6*

Calories: About 310 calories per serving.

Dynasty Beef on Green Cabbage

1 pound ground beef (or pork)
1 can (8 oz.) LA CHOY® Water Chestnuts, chopped fine
2 green onions, chopped fine
2 tablespoons minced fresh ginger
1 egg, lightly beaten
1½ teaspoons cornstarch
1 teaspoon sugar
½ teaspoon salt
Dash pepper (or to taste)
1 tablespoon sherry
Oil for deep frying
1 medium head green cabbage (or two heads celery or Chinese cabbage, if available)
2 tablespoons cooking oil
1 cup chicken broth, hot
1 tablespoon cornstarch
¼ cup chicken broth, cold

Combine meat, water chestnuts, green onions and ginger. Stir in egg, 1½ teaspoons cornstarch, sugar, salt, pepper and sherry; mix gently but thoroughly. Divide mixture into four parts; shape each part into a large meatball.

Heat oil in deep fryer or wok to 375 degrees. Using wire basket or strainer, lower meatballs into hot oil; deep fry until golden (about five minutes). Drain on paper towels. Pour off oil, straining and reserving for another use.

Cut cabbage into 8 sections. Heat 2 tablespoons oil in large skillet or wok placed over medium high heat. Add cabbage and cook, stirring constantly until softened. Transfer to large casserole, lining bottom and sides. Place meatballs on cabbage. Pour hot chicken broth over. Simmer, covered, about one hour or until meat is thoroughly cooked.

Using slotted spoon, arrange cabbage on serving platter; place meatballs on top. Blend remaining cornstarch and cold chicken broth; add to liquid remaining in casserole. Cook and stir over low heat until thickened. Pour sauce over meatballs; serve immediately. *4-6 servings*

Meatball Sukiyaki

1 pound ground beef
⅓ cup milk
⅓ cup fine dry bread crumbs
1 egg
1 teaspoon LAWRY'S® Seasoned Salt
1 package LAWRY'S® Brown Gravy Mix
1 tablespoon and 1 teaspoon sugar
1½ cups water
¼ cup soy sauce
1 cup diagonally cut celery
1½ cups diagonally cut green onions
¼ pound mushrooms, sliced
1 can (5 oz.) water chestnuts, sliced
1 quart (approximately 1 bunch) spinach leaves, torn in 2-inch pieces, stems removed

Combine ground beef, milk, bread crumbs, egg and **Seasoned Salt**. Form into meatballs about 1-inch diameter (makes about 30). Set aside.

Combine **Brown Gravy Mix**, sugar, water and soy sauce. Bring to a boil, stirring constantly. Reduce heat, add uncooked meatballs to gravy and simmer, uncovered, 10 minutes, stirring occasionally, to turn meatballs. Add celery, green onions, mushrooms and water chestnuts and simmer, covered, 5 minutes. Add spinach and simmer, covered 2 minutes longer until spinach wilts. Serve immediately with fluffy rice. *Makes 6 servings*

Chinese Meatballs with Veg-All® Mixed Vegetables

1 lb. ground beef chuck
⅛ tsp. pepper
2 eggs slightly beaten
3 Tbsp. salad oil
1½ cups beef broth or bouillon
1 Tbsp. soy sauce
1-16 oz. can VEG-ALL® Mixed Vegetables, drained
1 tsp. salt
½ cup dry bread crumbs
3 Tbsp. cornstarch
4 spring onions, chopped
½ lb. fresh mushrooms, sliced
1 Tbsp. cornstarch

Combine ground chuck, salt, pepper, bread crumbs and eggs; shape into 1½ inch balls. Roll in 3 tablespoons cornstarch. Place oil in heavy frying pan; sauté onions for approximately 2 minutes. Remove onions. Add meatballs to frying pan and cook over moderate heat, stirring constantly, until brown. Add beef broth and mushrooms; bring to a boil and cover tightly. Simmer for about 10 minutes. Mix soy sauce and 1 tablespoon cornstarch and stir into broth. Simmer over low heat until thick; add onions and **VEG-ALL®**. Simmer until heated. Serve hot. May be served with white rice or chow mein noodles. *Serves 6-8*

Rice Filled Teriyaki Meatloaf

Meatloaf:
2 lb. lean ground beef
6 tablespoons A.1. Steak Sauce
3 tablespoons *each* soy sauce and REGINA Cooking Sherry
1 tablespoon dark brown sugar
2 eggs, beaten
1 cup dry bread crumbs
1 medium clove garlic, crushed

Rice Filling:
1 medium onion, sliced
⅓ cup sliced celery
1 tablespoon butter (or margarine)
1 can (8 oz.) sliced water chestnuts, drained
½ cup drained bean sprouts
1 egg, beaten
⅔ cup rice, cooked
½ teaspoon salt

Lightly combine meatloaf ingredients. Set aside. In small saucepan, cook onion and celery in butter until onion is soft. Mix in remaining ingredients. Pat ½ meat mixture in 9 x 9 x 2-inch pan. Spread rice filling evenly over meat. Pat remaining meat carefully over filling. Bake in preheated 350° F oven 1 hour. Let stand 5 minutes. Cut in squares. *Makes 9 servings*

Sukiyaki

2 lb. lean ground beef
2 tablespoons sugar
⅓ cup Japanese soy sauce
¼ cup A.1. Steak Sauce
1 teaspoon salt
1 can (6 oz.) sliced mushrooms
2 medium onions, thinly sliced
1 green pepper, sliced in thin strips
6 scallions, cut in 1 inch pieces
1 cup thinly sliced celery
1 can (8 oz.) water chestnuts, thinly sliced
1 can (8 oz.) bamboo shoots
1 tablespoon cornstarch
1½ cups converted rice, cooked

In large skillet, brown beef until crumbly. In small bowl, mix sugar, soy sauce, **A.1.** and salt. Set aside. Drain mushrooms, reserving liquid. When meat is cooked, mix in vegetables. Add sauce. Simmer 3 minutes, or until vegetables are just tender crisp. Combine cornstarch and reserved mushroom liquid. Stir into Sukiyaki. Cook just until thickened. Serve over rice. *Serves 8*

Krispy® American Chopped Suey

½ pound ground lean beef
2 tablespoons shortening
⅓ cup diced onion
½ cup diced celery
1 (10½ ounce) can tomato puree
1 (8 ounce) can spaghetti sauce
2½ cups coarsely crushed SUNSHINE® KRISPY® Saltine Crackers
1 egg, beaten
1 cup grated American cheese
1 cup milk
2 tablespoons minced parsley
1 teaspoon salt

Heat oven to 325°F. Brown beef in shortening, breaking it with a spoon into small bits. Add onion, celery, tomato puree and spaghetti sauce. Cook, uncovered, over low heat for 20 minutes. Combine crushed cracker crumbs, beaten egg, grated cheese, milk, parsley and salt. Stir **KRISPY® Cracker** crumb mixture into tomato mixture. Pour into a greased 1½-quart baking dish. Bake, uncovered, at 325°F. for 40 minutes.

Yield: 4 to 5 generous servings

Hamburger Omelets Fu Yung

6 eggs, separated
¾ pound ground beef
1¼ teaspoons **LAWRY'S® Seasoned Salt**
½ teaspoon **LAWRY'S® Seasoned Pepper**
2 tablespoons minced parsley
½ cup minced onion
2 tablespoons butter

Beat egg yolks until thick and lemon colored. Blend in ground beef, **Seasoned Salt**, **Seasoned Pepper**, parsley and onion. Beat egg whites until stiff peaks form. Fold whites into meat mixture. Melt butter in electric skillet at 320°F. or in skillet over low heat. For each omelet use a scant ¼ cup. Cook about 3 minutes on each side or until browned. Use additional butter for frying if necessary. *Makes about 18*

Wild Rice Oriental Casserole

1 cup **CHIEFTAIN Wild Rice,** raw
1 lb. ground beef, cooked and drained
1 can cream of mushroom soup
1 can whole mushrooms, drained
1 can water chestnuts, sliced
1 can bamboo shoots, drained
¼ cup soy sauce
1 small onion, chopped
¼ cup green pepper (optional)
½ cup celery, chopped

Cook wild rice as in basic preparation, add *no* salt to water. Sauté onion, celery and green pepper. Combine all ingredients. Bake in 350° oven for 45 min. *Serves 6-8*

Teriyaki Burgers

1 can (8¼ oz.) pineapple slices
3 tablespoons soy sauce
1 tablespoon catsup
½ teaspoon marjoram leaves, crushed
⅛ teaspoon garlic powder
¼ teaspoon ground ginger
¼ cup finely chopped onion
1 pound ground beef
1½ cups **RICE CHEX® Cereal** crushed to ½ cup
1½ teaspoons packed brown sugar, divided
1 tablespoon butter or margarine

Drain pineapple, reserving juice. In large bowl combine soy sauce, catsup and 1 tablespoon pineapple juice. Remove 3 tablespoons of mixture. Set aside.

To mixture in large bowl add marjoram, garlic powder and ginger. Blend well. Add onion, ground beef and **CHEX®** crumbs. Mix thoroughly. Shape into 6 patties. Add ½ teaspoon brown sugar to reserved soy sauce mixture. Grill or broil to desired doneness, brushing with reserved sauce.

Meanwhile, in medium-size skillet sauté pineapple slices in remaining 1 teaspoon brown sugar and butter. Serve on top burgers. *Makes 6 burgers*

Pork

Glazed Cantonese Ham Patties

¾ lb. ground ham
¼ lb. lean ground pork
¾ cup soft bread crumbs
¼ cup chopped onion
2 tablespoons chopped green pepper
½ cup **LA CHOY® Water Chestnuts,** chopped
½ teaspoon dry mustard
1½ teaspoons **LA CHOY® Soy Sauce**
1½ teaspoons prepared horseradish
2 tablespoons **LA CHOY® Sweet & Sour Sauce**
½ cup buttermilk
1 egg, beaten
Additional **LA CHOY® Sweet & Sour Sauce**
Pimiento strips

Combine ham, pork, bread crumbs, onion, green pepper, water chestnuts, dry mustard, soy sauce, horseradish, and Sweet & Sour Sauce. Add buttermilk and egg; mix lightly. Shape into eight patties. Bake at 350 degrees for 25 minutes. Brush tops lightly with additional Sweet & Sour Sauce; bake 5 minutes more. Garnish with pimiento strips. *8 servings*

Ham Egg Foo Yung

(Low Calorie)

4 eggs
1 cup bean sprouts
3 oz. (3 slices) **KAHN'S® Cooked Ham,** cut into small pieces
2 green onions, thinly sliced (approx. ¼ cup)
1 can (2½ oz.) sliced mushrooms
1 Tbsp. soy sauce
1 tsp. vegetable oil
Chinese Sauce* (optional)

22

Beat eggs well. Add bean sprouts, ham, green onions, mushrooms and soy sauce; mix well. Heat 1 tsp. oil in an 8-inch nonstick skillet. Pour in egg mixture. Scramble eggs until partially set; then press down on egg mixture with spatula to form appearance of an omelette. When evenly set, turn to brown other side. Invert onto serving plate. Serve with Chinese Sauce if desired.

Makes 2 servings

Calories: 246 calories per serving

*Chinese Sauce

2 tsp. cornstarch
½ cup beef broth
1 Tbsp. soy sauce

Mix all ingredients together and heat, stirring constantly. Boil 1 minute. Serve with Ham Egg Foo Yung.

Ham and Rice Stir-Fry

1 tsp. vegetable oil
5 slices (5 oz.) **KAHN'S® Cooked Ham**, cut into thin strips
1 can (8 oz.) sliced water chestnuts, drained
2 green onions, chopped (approx. ¼ cup)
2 tsp. soy sauce, divided
1 cup cooked rice
Chinese Sauce (optional; see recipe above)*

Heat oil in large nonstick skillet. Add ham, water chestnuts, green onions and 1 tsp. soy sauce. Cook over medium heat, stirring occasionally, until ham is browned and slightly crisp, about 10 minutes. Add cooked rice and remaining 1 tsp. soy sauce to ham mixture. Continue cooking until rice is heated through. Serve with Chinese Sauce if desired.

Makes 2 servings

Calories: 246 calories per serving

Grilled Ham Steaks Mandarin

4 ½-inch slices from 3-lb. **HORMEL BLACK LABEL® Ham**
2 Tbsp. cooking oil
1 medium onion, sliced
1 green pepper, cut in 1 inch chunks
13-oz. can pineapple chunks
1 cup chicken bouillon
¼ cup vinegar
¼ cup brown sugar
2 Tbsp. cornstarch
2 Tbsp. soy sauce
½ cup mandarin orange sections

Place cooking oil in small skillet; sauté green pepper and onion about 5 minutes; remove. Heat ½ cup of liquid from pineapple in

skillet with bouillon, brown sugar and vinegar. Add cornstarch and soy sauce, stirring constantly, until sauce thickens. Add fruit and vegetables; keep warm. Grill ham steaks 3 minutes per side. Serve with sweet sour mixture.

Sweet and Tangy Barbecued Spareribs

4 pounds pork spareribs, cut into serving-size pieces
1½ teaspoons salt
¼ cup honey
2 tablespoons **LEA & PERRINS Worcestershire Sauce**
2 tablespoons soy sauce
2 tablespoons catsup
2 tablespoons water

Sprinkle both sides of the ribs with salt. Place on a rack in a baking pan. Bake in a preheated very hot oven (450 F.) for 20 minutes, turning once. Reduce oven heat to moderate (350 F.). Cook until almost tender, about 20 minutes longer. To prepare barbecue sauce combine remaining ingredients; blend well. Brush over ribs. Cook 30 minutes longer, brushing and turning frequently.

Indonesian Barbecued Pork Spareribs

2 to 3 lb. country-style pork spareribs
½ cup finely chopped onion
1 clove garlic, minced
½ teaspoon ground coriander or 1 teaspoon fresh cilantro (coriander) leaves
1 teaspoon salt
¼ teaspoon black pepper
Dash cayenne pepper
2 teaspoons ground all-purpose chocolate
3 tablespoons lemon juice
2 tablespoons brown sugar
4 tablespoons soy sauce
1 tablespoon vegetable oil
1 can (8 oz.) pineapple chunks in unsweetened juice
2 to 3 tablespoons **BLUE RIBBON® Slivered Almonds**, toasted

Arrange spareribs in glass bowl or baking pan. Combine onion, garlic, coriander, salt, pepper, cayenne, chocolate, lemon juice, brown sugar, soy, oil and juice from the pineapple chunks; mix well and pour over spareribs, marinate several hours or overnight.

About 1½ hours before you plan to serve, ignite charcoal; let it burn down to ashen-red. On grill, barbecue ribs slowly, turning occasionally and brushing with marinade. Five to ten minutes before serving, heat remaining marinade; add pineapple and almonds and heat through. Serve sauce over ribs or in small bowls.

Makes 4 to 6 servings

Lipton.

Saucy Spareribs

1 envelope **LIPTON® Onion Soup Mix**
1½ cups water
⅓ cup honey
¼ cup soy sauce
2 tablespoons sherry
1 teaspoon ginger
4 pounds spareribs, cut into serving pieces

In large shallow baking dish, combine all ingredients except spareribs; add spareribs. Cover and marinate in refrigerator, turning occasionally, at least 3 hours.

Preheat oven to 350°. Remove spareribs, reserving marinade. Place ribs on rack in foil-lined baking dish. Bake, turning and basting occasionally with marinade, 1¼ hours or until spareribs are done. *Makes about 6 servings*

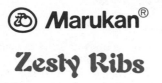

Zesty Ribs

5 lb. spareribs, cracked, cut in 3 rib portions
1 can (lb.) tomato sauce
¼ cup minced onion
2 Tbsp. soy sauce
1 tsp. salt
¼ tsp. pepper
¼ tsp. ground cloves
½ cup **MARUKAN® Seasoned Gourmet Rice Vinegar**
½ cup vegetable oil

Parboil spareribs. In medium bowl, combine tomato sauce, soy sauce, onion, salt, pepper and cloves with vinegar and oil. Place ribs in bowl and marinate for several hours. Broil, brushing frequently with marinade sauce, about 30 minutes until tender and crisp.

Apricot Barbecued Spareribs

2 large strips spareribs (about 3½ pounds), with bones cracked for easy handling
2 tablespoons olive or vegetable oil
1 medium-size onion, grated (¼ cup)
1 clove garlic, finely minced
½ cup honey
½ cup catsup
½ cup **COLONIAL CLUB Apricot Liqueur**
¼ cup Worcestershire sauce
1½ tablespoons soy sauce
1½ teaspoons dry mustard
1 tablespoon bottled meat concentrate
¼ teaspoon leaf oregano, crumbled
¼ teaspoon black pepper
Salt

Bake spareribs in moderate oven (350 degrees) for 45 minutes. Prepare sauce; combine oil, onion, garlic, honey, catsup, **COLONIAL CLUB Apricot Liqueur**, Worcestershire sauce, soy sauce, mustard, meat concentrate, oregano and pepper in large saucepan;

stir well and simmer for 30 minutes. Taste; add salt, if needed. Baste spareribs with sauce and bake at 350 degrees for 1 hour, basting several times during baking time.

Fuji Spareribs

1 can (29 ounce) cling peach slices
3 pounds lean pork spareribs, cut into 1-inch pieces
1 tablespoon vegetable oil
½ cup vinegar
⅓ cup brown sugar
2 tablespoons soy sauce
1 large clove garlic, crushed
1 teaspoon salt
1 bell pepper, sliced
2 tablespoons cornstarch

Drain peaches, saving ¾ cup peach syrup. Brown ribs in heavy skillet with vegetable oil until no longer pink. Drain excess oil. Add vinegar, syrup, brown sugar, soy sauce, garlic and salt. Bring to bubbling slow boil and reduce heat to medium low. Cover and cook 1½ hours. Before serving, add green pepper slices. Mix cornstarch with ¼ cup cold water, stirring into juices to thicken. Add peach slices. *Serves 6*

Favorite recipe from **Cling Peach Advisory Board**

Sweet & Sour Pork

1 can (20 oz.) **DOLE® Crushed Pineapple in Syrup**
1 lb. pork shoulder, cubed
2 tablespoons vegetable oil
1 cup sliced carrots
½ cup sliced green onions
½ cup chunked green bell pepper
¼ cup plum jam
2 tablespoons red wine vinegar
2 tablespoons soy sauce
1 tablespoon cornstarch
½ teaspoon ground ginger

Drain pineapple, reserving syrup. Brown pork in oil. Cover; simmer 20 minutes. Remove pork from skillet. Stir vegetables into pan drippings. Sauté just until tender. Remove from pan. Add plum jam; stir until melted. Add pineapple syrup, vinegar and soy sauce. Cook one minute. Stir a little sauce into cornstarch and ginger, mixing until smooth. Add to skillet. Cook until mixture is clear and thickened. Return pork, vegetables and pineapple to skillet. Toss lightly to coat with sauce. Serve with rice, if desired. *Makes 4 servings*

Sweet-Sour Pork Chops

6 rib pork chops, ½ inch thick
1 tablespoon shortening
Salt and pepper
½ cup catsup
½ cup pineapple juice
1 tablespoon brown sugar
1 tablespoon lemon juice
2 tablespoons minced onion
1 teaspoon Worcestershire sauce
½ teaspoon salt
⅛ teaspoon ground cloves
2 bags **SUCCESS® Rice**

Brown pork chops in shortening, drain excess fat. Sprinkle lightly with salt and pepper. Combine catsup and next 7 ingredients; pour over the pork chops. Cover; simmer 45 minutes, basting occasionally or until meat is tender. Skim excess fat from sauce.

Prepare rice according to package directions. Serve pork chops and sauce on bed of rice.

Sweet Sour Pork

Drain, reserving juice:
> 1 can (15¼ oz) **DEL MONTE Pineapple Chunks In Its Own Juice**

Thinly slice:
> ¾ cup onion
> ¾ cup green pepper
> ½ cup celery
> 1 lb. pork butt

Dissolve in reserved juice:
> 2 Tbsp. cornstarch

Add:
> ½ cup firmly packed brown sugar
> ½ cup water
> ⅓ cup vinegar
> 2 Tbsp. soy sauce
> 1 tsp. instant beef bouillon
> ⅛ tsp. ground ginger

Set aside. Heat in skillet or wok:
> 2 Tbsp. peanut or salad oil

Sauté pork, stirring constantly, until tender. Remove; set aside. Sauté vegetables, stirring constantly, until tender. Add pineapple chunks, pork and cornstarch mixture. Cook, stirring constantly, until sauce thickens and is translucent. Cover and keep warm. Serve over hot rice.

Sweet and Sour Pork with Cranberries

> 1 pound lean pork cut into 1 inch cubes
> Salt and pepper
> 1 egg
> ¼ cup cornstarch
> ¼ cup consommé
> 6 tablespoons flour
> Peanut oil, ½ inch deep
> ½ cup **OCEAN SPRAY® Cranberry Juice Cocktail**
> ½ cup **OCEAN SPRAY® Whole Berry Cranberry Sauce**
> 1 green pepper, diced
> 1 large onion, diced
> 2 zucchini, diced

Sprinkle pork cubes with salt and pepper. In a bowl, beat egg with cornstarch, consommé and flour. Dip pork into mixture. Fry pork in peanut oil until richly browned and cooked. Drain cubes on absorbent paper. In a saucepan, heat cranberry juice and cranberry sauce until smooth. Pour all of the oil out of the skillet leaving only 1 tablespoon in skillet. Sauté (over very high heat) green pepper in oil for 20 seconds. Add onion and sauté another 20 seconds. Add zucchini and sauté another 20 seconds. Stir in cranberry mixture. Add pork cubes and bring mixture just to a boil. Season to taste with salt and pepper. *Serves 4*

Sweet and Sour Pork

> 1 pound lean pork
> 2 Tbsp. **HOLLAND HOUSE® Sherry Cooking Wine**
> Salt to taste
> 1 Tbsp. cornstarch
> 2 Tbsp. oil
> 1 can (8 oz.) pineapple chunks
> 1 onion, thinly sliced
> ½ cup green peppers, thinly sliced
> 1 tomato, cut in wedges
> 6 water chestnuts, sliced
> 1 dozen peapods

Cut pork in one inch cubes. Mix sherry, salt and cornstarch. Add to pork cubes and marinate 10 minutes. Brown meat in hot oil.

Sauce for Sweet and Sour Pork:
> 2 Tbsp. cornstarch dissolved in ½ cup water
> ½ cup white vinegar
> ½ cup **COCO CASA™ Cream of Coconut**
> Salt to taste
> 2 Tbsp. soy sauce
> 1 cup pineapple juice

Stir together all sauce ingredients and cook, stirring until mixture is thick and clear. Add more cream of coconut if mixture is tart.

Add pork cubes to sauce and simmer, covered, for 1 hour or until meat is tender. Remove from heat and stir in pineapple chunks, onion, green pepper, tomato, water chestnuts and peapods. Heat to boiling and serve. *Serves 6 to 8*

Merlino's
Stir Fried Pork and Merlino's Fettuccine

> 8 ounces **MERLINO'S Fettuccine**
> 1 pound boneless pork—cut in thin strips, trimmed of fat (if meat is partially frozen, it is easier to cut into strips)
> 2 Tbsp. oil
> 6 whole green onions, sliced
> 1 tsp. ground ginger *or* 2 slices ginger root
> 1 clove minced garlic
> ½ tsp. pepper
> 1½ cups chicken broth (1 can undiluted chicken broth)
> 4 tsp. soy sauce
> 2 Tbsp. cornstarch
> ½ cup cold water
> ½ package frozen pea pods

Bring 4 quarts water to boil in large kettle. Meanwhile, in skillet, thoroughly brown pork in hot oil. Add onions, garlic, ginger and pepper. Stir in broth and soy sauce. Bring to a boil. Simmer for 10 minutes. Combine cornstarch and water, stir slowly into pork mixture. Cook until thickened. Add pea pods. Heat through. Cook the **MERLINO'S Fettuccine** as directed on package. Drain and serve immediately with pork sauce. *Serves 4*

PAM®

Mandarin Pork Stir-Fry

PAM® No-Stick Cooking Spray
1 pound lean pork, cut in strips
¼ pound fresh mushrooms, halved or cut in quarters
1 medium green pepper, cut in strips
1 small onion, chopped
1 cup water
2 teaspoons cornstarch
1 tablespoon soy sauce
1 chicken bouillon cube
½ teaspoon dry mustard
⅛ teaspoon garlic powder
1 can (8 ounces) water chestnuts, drained and sliced
1 orange, sectioned
Salt and pepper

Coat inside of large skillet or wok with **PAM® No-Stick Cooking Spray** according to directions; heat over medium heat. Cook and stir half the pork at a time until lightly browned. Remove to a plate. Reduce heat to low; add mushrooms, green pepper and onion. Cook and stir 3 minutes. Stir together ¼ cup water and cornstarch until smooth; mix in remaining water, soy sauce, bouillon cube, mustard and garlic powder. Add to skillet; cook and stir until mixture thickens and boils. Add meat and water chestnuts; simmer 3 minutes. Gently stir in orange sections; heat to serving temperature. Season to taste with salt and pepper.

Makes 4 servings

Calories per serving: 371

Oriental Pork and Vegetable Stir-Fry

2 pounds boneless pork shoulder, fat trimmed and cut in 2-inch strips
2 tablespoons dry sherry, divided
6 teaspoons soy sauce, divided
2 teaspoons AC'CENT® Brand Flavor Enhancer
¾ teaspoon ground ginger
4 tablespoons vegetable oil, divided
2 cloves garlic, crushed
2 cups diagonally sliced carrots
2 cups diagonally sliced celery
4 scallions, cut in 1-inch pieces
3 cups shredded fresh spinach
½ cup dry roasted peanuts
½ cup water
1½ teaspoons cornstarch
¼ teaspoon sugar

In large bowl combine pork, 1 tablespoon sherry, 2 teaspoons soy sauce, **AC'CENT®** and ginger; marinate 15 minutes. In wok or large skillet heat 2 tablespoons oil with garlic. Add carrots; stir-fry 2 to 3 minutes. Add celery and scallions; stir-fry 2 minutes longer. Add spinach and peanuts; stir-fry 1 minute longer. Remove from wok and set aside. Heat remaining 2 tablespoons oil. Stir-fry pork until lightly browned, 5 to 7 minutes. In small bowl combine water, remaining 4 teaspoons soy sauce, 1 tablespoon sherry,

cornstarch and sugar. Add to wok. Cook until sauce thickens slightly. Return vegetables; heat through. Serve with rice, if desired.

Yield: 6 servings

Stir-Fry Pork with Cabbage and Chinese Celery Cabbage

2 Tablespoons soy sauce
1 Tablespoon dry sherry cooking wine
¼ teaspoon monosodium glutamate
1 pound lean pork, cut in 2 x ½-inch strips
¼ cup salad oil
½ cup thinly sliced celery
5 cups 1-inch pieces cabbage (1 to 1½ pounds small head)
2 cups 1-inch pieces Chinese celery cabbage (1 pound medium head)
½ cup water
1 Tablespoon cornstarch
½ teaspoon salt
¼ teaspoon monosodium glutamate
½ cup water
1 Tablespoon soy sauce

Combine 2 Tablespoons soy sauce, sherry and monosodium glutamate; pour over pork. Heat oil in large skillet. Put in pork mixture and stir about 3 to 4 minutes or until pork is well cooked. Remove pork to warm plate leaving as much oil as possible in skillet.

Add sliced celery, cabbage and Chinese celery cabbage gradually to hot skillet as much as can fit. Add and stir until all vegetables are just wilted. Add ½ cup water, cover and simmer for 10 minutes or until tender. Stir occasionally. Return pork pieces to skillet.

Mix together cornstarch, salt and ¼ teaspoon monosodium glutamate, ½ cup water and 1 Tablespoon soy sauce. Stir into cabbage mixture. Heat and stir until mixture thickens. Serve hot.

Makes 4 to 6 servings

Favorite recipe from **Leafy Greens Council**

Chinese Pork and Vegetable Stir-Fry

1 lb. **JOHN MORRELL® TABLE TRIM® Boneless Fresh Pork Loin End,** cut into thin bite-sized strips
1 Tbsp. cornstarch
½ tsp. ground ginger
2 tsp. sugar
2 Tbsp. dry sherry
2 Tbsp. soy sauce
½ cup chicken broth
4 Tbsp. cooking oil
6 oz. frozen package pea pods, partially thawed
1 lb. can mixed Chinese Vegetables, drained
1 sweet red pepper, cut into ¼ in. strips (or tomato)
Hot cooked rice

In small bowl, combine cornstarch, ginger, sugar, sherry, soy sauce, and chicken broth. Set aside. Heat 2 Tbsp. oil in 12 in. skillet or wok pan. Add vegetables, and stir-fry 2 to 3 minutes. Remove vegetables, set aside. Add remaining oil, and pork strips. Stir-fry until pork is well browned—4 to 5 minutes. Add vegetables, and soy sauce mixture to pork. Stir to blend. Heat until sauce is bubbly. Serve at once over hot, fluffy rice.   *Serves 4*

Stir Fry Wild Rice, Snow Peas and Pork

½ pound pork tenderloin, sliced ¼ inch thick
3 tablespoons vegetable oil
1 cup sliced celery
1 cup sliced green onion
1 cup sliced fresh mushrooms
1 can (8 oz.) water chestnuts, sliced
½ pound snow peas or edible pod peas, fresh or frozen, thawed
1 tablespoon grated fresh ginger root
2 cups cooked **CHIEFTAIN** Wild Rice
1 tablespoon cornstarch
1 tablespoon dry sherry
¼ cup soy sauce
½ teaspoon salt
½ teaspoon salted cashews or sunflower nuts

Slice pork and set aside. Heat oil in heavy skillet; add pork and stir-fry over high heat for 2 minutes until meat is no longer pink. Add celery, green onion, mushrooms, water chestnuts, pea pods and ginger and stir-fry for 5 minutes over high heat until vegetables are tender crisp. Toss in the wild rice until evenly blended. Mix cornstarch with sherry, soy sauce and salt, add to juices in pan and cook about a minute until thickened. Toss mixture together to coat everything with glaze. Garnish with cashews.   *Serves 4*

Pork Chow Mein

1 lb. **WILSON®** Recipe Ready Brand Boneless Pork Tenderloin
2 tablespoons soy sauce
⅛ teaspoon ground ginger
4 green onions, cut in 1 inch pieces
¼ cup oil
½ cup sliced celery
1 cup thinly sliced mushrooms
½ cup julienne carrots
1 cup French cut green beans
1 tablespoon cornstarch
¾ cup chicken broth
8 oz. Chinese egg noodles (or regular egg noodles if you cannot find Chinese), cooked

Cut tenderloin in ¼ inch thick slices. Combine 1 tablespoon soy sauce and ginger in a small bowl. Add pork and green onions.

Toss to mix. Let stand 10 minutes. Heat 2 tablespoons oil in a large skillet or a wok over high heat. Add pork and cook and stir until meat loses its pink color. Remove from pan. Add remaining 2 tablespoons oil. Add celery, mushrooms, carrots and green beans. Cook and stir 3 minutes. Return meat to pan. Combine 1 tablespoon soy sauce and cornstarch. Stir in chicken broth. Stir into vegetable mixture. Heat, stirring constantly, until mixture comes to a full boil. Reduce heat and cook 3 to 5 minutes or until pork is done. Serve over egg noodles.   *Makes 4 servings*

Stir-Fry Pork with Vegetables

1 pound boneless pork blade steak
½ pound fresh broccoli
½ pound carrots
¼ cup water
2 tablespoons soy sauce
1 tablespoon sugar
1 teaspoon cornstarch
2 tablespoons cooking oil
1 teaspoon garlic salt
Hot cooked rice
Additional soy sauce, optional

Cut pork into ⅛-inch thick strips. Cut broccoli stems into ⅛-inch thick slices and separate the flowerets. Cut carrots into ⅛-inch thick diagonal slices. Combine water, soy sauce, sugar and cornstarch; stir until free of lumps. Heat 1 tablespoon oil in Chinese wok or 10-inch skillet over medium high heat. Add broccoli stems and carrots; cook and stir until vegetables are hot but crisp, 2-3 minutes. Add broccoli flowerets; cook and stir 1 minute. Remove vegetables from wok or skillet. Add remaining 1 tablespoon oil to wok or skillet; heat over high heat. Add pork strips; cook and stir 4-5 minutes or until meat is lightly browned and tender, stirring constantly. Add soy sauce mixture; cook until sauce is thickened and clear, stirring constantly. Add broccoli and carrots. Sprinkle with garlic salt; stir and heat. Serve immediately over rice with additional soy sauce, if desired.   *Makes 4 servings*

Favorite recipe from **National Pork Producers Council**

Cantonese Pork Chops

6 loin pork chops, 1-inch thick
2 tablespoons salad oil
1 can (30 ounces) apricot halves
½ cup water
2 to 3 tablespoons soy sauce
1 large clove garlic, crushed
½ teaspoon powdered ginger
1 can (8 ounces) water chestnuts, drained and sliced
5 scallions, sliced
2 cups diagonally sliced celery
Salt and pepper

Brown chops on both sides in hot oil in large skillet. Pour off excess fat. Drain syrup from apricots into skillet and add water, soy sauce, garlic and ginger. Cover and simmer 35 minutes; if necessary, add more water during cooking period. Add water chestnuts, scallions and celery; cook about 5 minutes more until celery is tender. Add apricots and cook just until heated through. Season sauce to taste with salt and pepper.   *Makes 6 servings*

Favorite recipe from **California Apricot Advisory Board**

Penang Pork Chops

2 tablespoons red wine vinegar
1 tablespoon FRENCH'S® Worcestershire Sauce
½ teaspoon FRENCH'S® Lemon Peel
½ teaspoon FRENCH'S ® Tarragon Leaves
½ teaspoon FRENCH'S® Thyme Leaves
2 dashes FRENCH'S® Cayenne Pepper
⅛ teaspoon FRENCH'S® Ground Nutmeg
2 tablespoons oil
¾ cup chicken broth
4 to 6 pork chops, cut ¾ to 1 inch thick
Cooked rice
Strips of fresh lemon peel, if desired

Combine vinegar, Worcestershire sauce, lemon peel, tarragon, thyme, cayenne, nutmeg, 1 tablespoon oil, and chicken broth; pour over chops and refrigerate 1 to 2 hours. Drain chops, reserving marinade. Brown chops in remaining oil in skillet; pour off excess fat. Add marinade and simmer, covered, 50 minutes, or until tender. Serve on rice, garnished with strips of fresh lemon peel. *4 to 6 servings*

MICROWAVE METHOD:
Prepare marinade *reducing chicken broth to ¼ cup* and *oil to 1 tablespoon. Sprinkle chops with ¼ to ½ teaspoon salt.* Place chops, meaty side out, in shallow casserole; marinate. Cover with plastic wrap and microwave on MEDIUM 10 minutes. Rearrange chops with pink areas facing out. Recover and microwave 6 minutes. Rearrange chops again and microwave 2 to 10 minutes or until chops are no longer pink near the bone.

Roast Pork with Orange Glaze

1 cup orange juice
1 tsp. curry powder
½ cup ESTEE® Granulated Fructose
2 cloves crushed garlic
Black pepper, freshly ground
¼ cup corn oil
4 lb. pork shoulder, boneless butt
Water
3 Tbsp. cornstarch

Mix first six ingredients together in small bowl. Trim excess fat from pork roast. Place roast in plastic bag or shallow pan, and cover with the marinade. Let meat marinade in refrigerator one to three hours.

Set oven to 375°F. Remove roast from marinade and place on rack in open roasting pan. Pour ½ cup water into bottom of pan. Baste roast with ¼ cup marinade every 30 minutes for first hour. Add more water to roasting pan when needed. Cover meat with foil when it becomes very brown and crispy, and lower oven temperature to 350° F. Cook for 45 minutes per pound, or until internal temperature is 185°F.

Remove roast from oven. Chill drippings and skim fat. Mix ½ cup water and 3 Tbsp. cornstarch until blended. Reheat gravy, and gradually add cornstarch. Heat until thickened. Serve gravy with sliced meat. Season to taste with **ESTEE® Salt-Free Meat Seasoning**.

Makes 12 servings, 3 oz. meat + 2 Tbsp. gravy per serving

NUTRITION INFORMATION

Calories	Carbohydrates	Protein	Fat	Cholesterol	Sodium
190	10g	21g	8g	120mg	55mg

DIABETIC EXCHANGE INFORMATION

Fruit	Meat
1	3

Pork Stew Oriental

1 pound (1 inch cubes) pork shoulder
1 to 2 tablespoons shortening
1¼ cups water
1 medium onion, quartered
Dash pepper
3 medium carrots, cut in ½ inch diagonal slices
1½ cups diagonally sliced celery
1 can (8 ounces) water chestnuts, halved
1 jar (12 ounces) HEINZ Home Style Pork Gravy
2 tablespoons soy sauce
1 tablespoon cornstarch
1 tablespoon water

Brown pork in shortening; drain excess fat. Add water, onion and pepper. Cover; simmer 45 minutes. Add carrots, celery and water chestnuts; stir in gravy and soy sauce. Cover; simmer an additional 20 minutes or until meat and vegetables are tender. Thicken with a mixture of cornstarch and water. Serve stew in a bowl topped with chow mein noodles or a mound of rice, if desired.

Makes 4-5 servings (about 5½ cups)

Pork with Mandarin Sauce, Made with Stock Mandarino Liqueur

2 cups roast pork, cut in long, thin strips (julienne)

Sauce:
One tablespoon cornstarch
½ cup orange juice
¼ cup gin
¼ cup STOCK Mandarino Liqueur
Four teaspoons soy sauce
One teaspoon vinegar
Two teaspoons honey
¼ teaspoon Chinese five-flavor spice (or a pinch each of ginger, cloves, cinnamon)
¼ teaspoon pepper
½ teaspoon garlic powder

Put cornstarch into a saucepan. Slowly add orange juice and stir until smooth. Add other sauce ingredients. Cook about five minutes over medium heat, stirring constantly, until thickened. Add pork strips and cook about three minutes more until heated through. Serve over rice. *Serves four*

Kiwifruit Teriyaki Pork

Place a loin of boneless pork on a rack in a shallow pan. Rub with salt and pepper. Sprinkle on rosemary. Roast at 350° for 2-2½ hours. Mix ½ cup each of ketchup and soy sauce, ¼ cup honey, 1 crushed garlic clove. Use as basting last 45 minutes.

Transfer to a heated platter. Surround meat with **CALAVO®** **Kiwifruit** slices and halves. Garnish with banana or ti leaves.

Tangy Pork Kabobs

1 **JOHN MORRELL® TABLE TRIM® Pork**
  Tenderloin, cut horizontally into 8, 1 inch pieces
Large, whole fresh mushrooms
Green pepper squares
Red sweet pepper squares *or*
  whole tomatoes, quartered
Par-boiled onions, quartered
½ cup chili sauce
¼ cup sugar
2 Tbsp. lemon juice
2 tsp. Worcestershire sauce
½ to 1 tsp. chili powder
Hot cooked rice

Thread pork pieces onto 2 skewers, leaving space between each so they will cook evenly. Thread alternating pieces of green pepper, red pepper, mushrooms and onions onto 2 separate skewers. Blend together remaining ingredients except rice. Spread on meat and vegetables. Place pork kabobs on broiler rack in pan and broil 3 to 4 inches from heat for 20 to 25 minutes, or until done. Baste meat frequently with sauce, turning several times. During the last 10 minutes, place vegetable kabobs on broiler rack. Turn once and baste with sauce. Serve pork and vegetable kabobs over hot cooked rice. *Serves 3-4*

Sausage

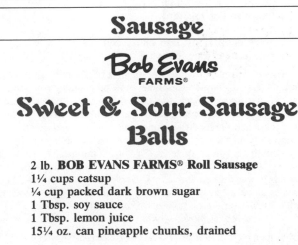

Sweet & Sour Sausage Balls

2 lb. **BOB EVANS FARMS® Roll Sausage**
1¼ cups catsup
¼ cup packed dark brown sugar
1 Tbsp. soy sauce
1 Tbsp. lemon juice
15¼ oz. can pineapple chunks, drained

About 50 minutes before serving: Shape sausage into 1-inch balls. In large skillet over medium heat, brown sausage balls one-half at a time until lightly browned. Drain on paper towels. Drain skillet.

Return all sausage balls to skillet; add catsup, brown sugar, soy sauce, lemon juice and ¼ cup water. Simmer, covered, 10 minutes stirring occasionally. Add pineapple chunks. Simmer, covered, until heated through. *Serves 6*

Oriental Sausage

1 green pepper, chunked
1 medium onion, chopped
3 small tomatoes, quartered
1 lb. **HILLSHIRE FARM® Smoked Sausage,** cut into
  ½ inch pieces
1 Tbsp. butter or margarine
1 Tbsp. cornstarch
½ tsp. ground ginger
1 Tbsp. vinegar
1 Tbsp. soy sauce
½ cup apricot preserves
2 cups drained pineapple chunks

Sauté green pepper, onion, tomato, and sausage in butter for 5 minutes. Combine cornstarch, ginger, vinegar, soy sauce and preserves. Stir into sausage mixture. Cook over low heat until sauce thickens. Mix in pineapple chunks and heat. Serve with rice or Chinese noodles. *Yield: 6 servings*

Tropical Kabobs

1 lb. **JIMMY DEAN® Special Recipe Sausage**
1 small can (8½ oz.) sliced pineapple, drained (reserve syrup)
1 Tbsp. brown sugar
1 Tbsp. vinegar
1 Tbsp. soy sauce
1 tsp. cornstarch
4 green onions, cut into 2-inch pieces
1 green pepper, cut into 2-inch pieces

Shape sausage into 24 balls. Place in glass bowl. Mix reserved pineapple syrup, brown sugar, vinegar and soy sauce until sugar is dissolved. Pour over meatballs and refrigerate at least 3 hours.

Drain marinade from meatballs into small saucepan; stir in cornstarch. Cook, stirring constantly, until mixture thickens and boils. Boil and stir 1 minute. Remove sauce from heat and set aside.

Cut pineapple slices into quarters. On each of six metal skewers, alternate 4 meatballs with pineapple pieces and vegetables; brush kabobs with part of sauce. Grill over medium fire for 20 minutes. Brush occasionally with sauce and gently push with fork to turn. Serve with rice.

Golden Apple Stir-Fry

Stir-frying gives this entree an added crunch. Stir-fry 6 cups shredded cabbage (1 small head) 1 minute in 1 or 2 tablespoons oil. Sprinkle with 1 tablespoon vinegar, 1 teaspoon salt, ¼ teaspoon sugar and dash pepper. Add 1 chopped Golden Delicious apple and ½ pound smoky link sausages, halved. Cover and simmer 3 minutes or until links are heated and cabbage is cooked to desired degree tenderness. *Makes 4 servings*

Favorite recipe from **Washington State Apple Commission**

Lamb & Veal

Veal with Green Peppers and Black Mushrooms

A. Thinly slice:
    ½ lb. veal cutlet
B. Cut in matchstick shreds:
    6 soaked **CHINA BOWL® Black Mushrooms***
    1 large, seeded green pepper
C. Finely chop:
    1 clove garlic
    3 slices **CHINA BOWL® Fresh Ginger**
D. Mix chow sauce in a bowl:
    2 Tbsp. **CHINA BOWL® Chinese Light Soy Sauce**
    2 Tbsp. **CHINA BOWL® Chinese Cooking Wine** or dry sherry
    1 tsp. sugar
    1 tsp. corn starch
    ½ tsp. salt
    ¼ tsp. **CHINA BOWL® Taste Powder-MSG** (optional)
E. Cooking: Pour 2 Tbsp. peanut or vegetable oil into a wok or large skillet over high heat and, as oil starts to smoke, add garlic and ginger and stir fry for 30 seconds. Add veal and stir fry for 2 minutes more. Stir chow sauce, add to wok along with vegetables, reduce flame to medium and stir fry for 2 minutes.

Optional: Add ¼ tsp. **CHINA BOWL® Sesame Oil** just before completing cooking. Serves 4 when included in a Chinese family-style meal of 2 other main dishes and rice.

*These dried mushrooms will keep indefinitely when stored in a covered jar or closed plastic bag in a dry, cool place.

Note: This dish is equally good with pork or beef, but substitute **CHINA BOWL® Dark Soy Sauce** for the **Light** when making chow sauce.

Kikko Lamb Kabobs

½ cup wine vinegar
¼ cup **KIKKOMAN Soy Sauce**
2 tablespoons vegetable oil
2 teaspoons instant minced onion
1 clove garlic, crushed
¼ teaspoon pepper
1½ pounds fresh lamb shoulder, cut into 2-inch cubes

Combine vinegar, soy sauce, oil, onion, garlic and pepper in saucepan; bring to boil. Cool thoroughly; stir in lamb and marinate

2 to 3 hours. Arrange lamb on skewers; brush with marinade. Broil or grill to desired doneness, brushing with marinade.
Makes 4 servings

Lamb and Kumquat Kabobs

2 tablespoons butter or margarine
1 large onion, finely chopped
1 (10 ounce) jar **RAFFETTO® Preserved Kumquats**
1 teaspoon salt
2 tablespoons lemon juice
1 tablespoon soy sauce
2½ pounds lean leg of lamb, cut into 1 inch cubes

Melt butter or margarine in a saucepan. Add onion and cook until onion is limp but not browned. Add kumquats with liquid, salt, lemon juice and soy sauce. Add lamb and toss lightly. Refrigerate several hours or overnight. Stir occasionally. Thread meat and kumquats on skewers at least 6 inches long. Place on broiler pan and broil, about 10 minutes, turning once, or to desired degree of doneness. Brush with sauce during cooking time. *6 servings*

Note: If desired add squares of green peppers and button mushrooms to meat. Broil meat on separate skewers and broil kumquats, peppers and mushrooms on separate skewers, brushing both with marinade and cooking vegetables for half the length of time that the meat is cooked.

Fish & Shellfish

True Cod Kabobs, Teriyaki

2 pounds true cod or other thick fish fillets, fresh or frozen
1 can (16 ounces) pineapple chunks
¼ cup reserved pineapple juice
½ cup soy sauce
¼ cup sherry, optional
2 tablespoons brown sugar
1 tablespoon fresh-grated ginger root or 1 teaspoon ground ginger
1 teaspoon dry mustard
1 clove garlic, crushed
1 green pepper, cut into 1-inch squares
3 cups cooked rice, optional

Thaw fish if frozen. Cut into one-inch cubes. Drain pineapple; reserve ¼ cup of liquid. Combine pineapple juice, soy sauce, sherry, brown sugar, ginger, mustard, and garlic. Pour marinade over fish; cover and refrigerate for at least one hour. Drain fish and reserve marinade. Thread fish, pineapple chunks, and green pepper alternately on skewers. Cook over hot coals or under broiler, 4 to 5 inches from source of heat, for 4 to 5 minutes. Baste with marinade. Turn and cook for 4 to 5 minutes longer or until fish flakes easily when tested with a fork. Serve as a main dish on a bed of rice or alone as an hors d'oeuvre. For an extra festive touch, impale a flower on the end of each skewer after cooking.

Makes 6 entree servings or 18 to 20 hors d'oeurves

Favorite recipe from **National Marine Fisheries Service**

Fish Teriyaki

1-14 oz./397 g pkg. **HIGH LINER®** Fillets
3 ml dry mustard
3 ml water
75 ml dry white wine
15 ml Worcestershire sauce
1 ml ground ginger

Combine dry mustard and water; let stand 10 minutes. Add wine, Worcestershire sauce and ginger. Brush over frozen fillets. Bake in 230°C oven for 15-20 minutes or until fish flakes easily with fork. Baste with sauce while cooking. For added flavor, prepare the sauce and marinate fillets in it for 2-3 hours before cooking, keeping in mind that the cooking time will decrease as fillets thaw. To serve, sprinkle with paprika or parsley flakes.   *Serves 3-4*

Ginger Teriyaki Fish

2 pounds firm-fleshed fish, such as sea bass or snapper
½ cup chicken-flavor bouillon or stock
¼ cup dry sherry
1 tablespoon soy sauce
½ teaspoon grated fresh gingerroot
2 teaspoons cornstarch
1 tablespoon water
1 packet **SWEET 'N LOW®**
1 tablespoon Dijon mustard

Preheat broiler. Spray rack over broiler pan with non-stick coating agent. Wipe fish with paper towel and place on broiler rack. In small saucepan, combine bouillon, sherry, soy sauce, and ginger; bring to simmering over moderate heat. Combine cornstarch with water and add to sauce. Stir until mixture thickens; remove from heat. Stir in **SWEET 'N LOW®**. Brush fish with ¼ cup sauce. Broil 6 to 8 minutes, brushing fish twice with sauce. Fish is cooked when it flakes easily with a fork. Mix mustard with remaining sauce and serve over fish.   *6 servings*

PER SERVING (5 ounces): Calories: 170 Protein: 31gm
Carbohydrate: 3gm   Fat: 2gm   Sodium: 445mg

Japanese Stir-Fry Fish

1 tablespoon soy sauce
1 tablespoon sherry wine or water
2 teaspoons cornstarch
1 package (12 oz.) frozen flounder fillets, thawed and cut in strips*
2 tablespoons oil
1 package (10 oz.) **BIRDS EYE®** Japanese Style Stir-Fry Vegetables
1 small garlic clove, crushed

Combine soy sauce, sherry and cornstarch. Add fish and mix to coat all strips. Let stand for 10 minutes. Sauté fish in oil in large skillet for 1 or 2 minutes; keep warm. Prepare vegetables in separate clean skillet as directed on package, adding garlic with the vegetables. Arrange fish in center.

Makes 3¾ cups or 3 servings

*Or use ¾ pound fish fillets, cut in strips.

Pan Fried Fillets with Ginger Sauce

1 package **VAN DE KAMP'S® Today's Catch Cod** or **Fish Fillets**
2 Tbsp. oil
1 tsp. minced fresh ginger
1 green onion, thinly sliced
3 Tbsp. shredded or diced bamboo shoots
⅛ tsp. five-spice powder
2 tsp. cornstarch
½ cup chicken stock
3 Tbsp. soy sauce
2 tsp. sherry

Heat oil in skillet or wok and fry fillets 5 minutes on each side until light golden. Remove from heat and sprinkle ginger, green onion, bamboo shoots and five-spice powder over fish. Dissolve cornstarch in chicken stock, soy sauce and sherry. Pour over fish and bring quickly to a boil. Cover and simmer gently for 5 minutes. Serve with steamed rice.   *Serves 2*

Calories: 225 calories per servings.

Elegant Fish and Rice

1½ lb. tilefish fillets or other fish fillets, fresh or frozen
¾ teaspoon salt
¼ teaspoon pepper
2 tablespoons margarine or butter
¾ cup chopped celery
2 tablespoons chopped onion
2 cups cooked brown or white rice
1 can (16 ounces) green beans, drained
1 teaspoon salt
½ teaspoon thyme leaves
1 can (16 ounces) peach slices, drained; reserve ¾ cup syrup
¼ cup white wine
1 tablespoon cornstarch
2 teaspoons soy sauce
¼ teaspoon ground mace

Thaw fish if frozen. Sprinkle fish with ¾ teaspoon salt and pepper. In a 10-inch skillet, melt margarine. Sauté celery and onion until tender. Stir in rice, green beans, 1 teaspoon salt and thyme. Turn mixture into a baking dish, 12 × 7 × 2-inches. Arrange fillets on top of rice. Cover; bake in moderate oven, 350 degrees, for 20 minutes. Meanwhile, stir reserved peach syrup, wine, soy sauce and mace into cornstarch; cook and stir until thick and bubbly. Arrange peach slices around fish. Spoon wine sauce over all. Bake, uncovered 5 to 10 minutes more or until fish flakes easily when tested with a fork.   *Makes 4 servings*

Favorite recipe from **Florida Department of Natural Resources**

FLORIDA®
Gold and Silver Treasure Fish

1 teaspoon cornstarch
1½ tablespoons soy sauce
1½ tablespoons salad oil
1 tablespoon sherry
1 teaspoon sugar
½ teaspoon salt
¼ teaspoon pepper
3 tablespoons chopped scallions
1 clove garlic, minced
½ teaspoon finely chopped pared ginger root, or
    ¼ teaspoon ground ginger
1 cup Florida orange sections (about 4 oranges)
1 cup Florida grapefruit sections
1 package (6 ounces) frozen snow peas, thawed and
    drained
1 pound sea bass fillets, or other white fish fillets, cut
    in 1-inch cubes

In large bowl blend cornstarch and soy sauce. Stir in remaining ingredients. Cover and marinate in refrigerator at least 1 hour. Turn into 2-quart baking dish. Bake in 425°F. oven 12 to 15 minutes, or until fish flakes easily when tested with a fork. Serve over rice, if desired. *Yield: 4 servings*

Favorite recipe from **Florida Department of Citrus**

Chinese Tuna

1 can (1 lb.) chop suey vegetables
1 can (7 oz.) tuna, broken into chunks
1 can (8 oz.) water chestnuts, drained, sliced
2 tablespoons lemon juice
2 tablespoons soy sauce
¼ teaspoon ground ginger
4 teaspoons **ARGO®/KINGSFORD'S® Corn Starch**

Drain vegetables; reserve liquid. In medium skillet stir together ⅔ cup of the reserved liquid, vegetables, tuna, water chestnuts, lemon juice, soy sauce and ginger. Stirring occasionally, cook over medium heat 5 to 7 minutes or until heated through. Stir together corn starch and 4 teaspoons of the reserved liquid. Stir into skillet. Stirring constantly, bring to boil over medium heat and boil 1 minute. Serve with Chinese noodles.

Makes 3 to 4 servings

Oriental Casserole

1 3-oz. can chow mein noodles
1 can cream of mushroom soup
¼ cup water
1 can chunk tuna
Salt and pepper to taste
⅓ cup **FISHER'®S Cashew Nuts**
1 cup diced celery
¼ cup diced onion
¼ cup chopped green pepper

Oven 325°. Set aside ½ cup noodles. Combine remaining noodles with other ingredients and place in 1½ quart casserole. Sprinkle

with ½ cup reserved noodles and some of the cashew nuts. Bake at 325° for 40 minutes.

Tuna Lo-Mein

2 tablespoons vegetable oil*
1 cup scallions, cut into 2-inch pieces
1 cup thinly sliced red pepper
1 clove garlic, minced
2 cups sliced Chinese cabbage
1 can (16 ounces) bean sprouts, rinsed in cold water,
    drained
½ pound mushrooms, sliced
½ can (8 ounces) water chestnuts, drained and sliced
2 tablespoons soy sauce
½ teaspoon ground ginger
2 cups cooked fine noodles or thin spaghetti
2 cans (6½ or 7 ounces each) tuna, drained

In large skillet (or wok), heat oil over medium-high heat; stir-fry scallions, pepper and garlic, until crisp-tender. Add Chinese cabbage, bean sprouts, mushrooms and water chestnuts; stir-fry 2 minutes longer. Combine soy sauce and ginger, add to skillet. Stir in noodles and tuna; heat through. *Yield: 4 to 6 servings*

*If desired, for additional flavor and enrichment, drained oil from tuna may be substituted.

Favorite recipe from **Tuna Research Foundation**

Mandarin Tuna and Cashews

⅓ cup sugar
2 tablespoons cornstarch
½ teaspoon ground ginger
½ cup sherry
⅓ cup soy sauce
⅓ cup water
2 tablespoons cider vinegar
5 tablespoons vegetable oil, divided
1 clove garlic, minced
4 green onions, thinly sliced
1 large green pepper, cut into ½-inch pieces
1 cup celery, cut into ½-inch pieces
1 can (8 oz.) sliced water chestnuts, drained
¾ cup dry roasted whole cashews
1 can (13 oz.) **CHICKEN OF THE SEA® Solid
    White Tuna, drained***
Chow mein noodles

In small bowl combine sugar, cornstarch and ginger. Blend in sherry, soy sauce, water, vinegar and 2 tablespoons oil. Set aside.
  In large skillet or wok heat remaining 3 tablespoons oil. Add garlic, onions, green pepper, celery and water chestnuts. Stir-fry** 3 minutes. Add cashews. Stir-fry 1 minute. Reduce heat to medium. Stir soy sauce mixture. Add to skillet. Gently stir in tuna. Bring to a boil. Heat and stir until thickened and glossy. Serve over noodles. *Makes 4 to 5 servings*

*Tuna packed in oil or water may be used, based on personal preference.

**Cook and stir over high heat.

Oriental Broccoli and Bean Sprout Salad *(top)*, Chinese Imperial Chicken *(bottom)*
La Choy® *(La Choy Food Products)*

Menehune Chicken *(right)*, Teriyaki Meat Sticks *(left)*
Kikkoman *(Kikkoman International, Inc.)*

Ginger Pork Balls in Sherry-Orange Sauce
The Christian Brothers® *(Fromm and Sichel, Inc.)*

Chinese Spring Rolls
Dole® *(Castle & Cooke Foods)*

Sour Cream Teriyaki Dip *(top)*, Spicy Cocktail Dip *(middle)*, Creamy Mustard Dip *(bottom)*
Jeno's® *(Jeno's)*

Teriyaki Tidbits
Cookin' Good™ *(Showell Farms)*

Sashimi
Kikkoman *(Kikkoman International, Inc.)*

34

Chinese Barbecued Pork (Char Siu)
Kikkoman *(Kikkoman International, Inc.)*

Wheat Germ Egg Rolls
Kretschmer *(International Multifoods)*

Chicken Kabobs (Yakitori) *(bottom)*, Shrimp with Sweet-Sour
Sauce *(top)*
Kikkoman *(Kikkoman International, Inc.)*

35

Coriander Chicken Salad *(left)*, Wok-ie Talkie *(right)*
(California Iceberg Lettuce Commission)

Oriental Cauliflower Medley
Land O Lakes® *(Land O'Lakes, Inc.)*

Sweet-and-Sour Potato Medley
Betty Crocker® *(General Mills, Inc.)*

Sweet 'n Sour Stir Fry
Wish-Bone® *(Thomas J. Lipton, Inc.)*

Oriental Sprout Salad
Oscar Mayer *(Oscar Mayer Foods Corporation)*

Oriental Tuna Salad
Betty Crocker® **Tuna Helper**® *(General Mills, Inc.)*

Japanese Pickled Cauliflower
Coca-Cola® *(The Coca-Cola Company)*

Lite Spinach Salad
Del Monte *(Del Monte Corporation)*

Chinese Pork and Vegetable Stir-Fry
John Morrell® Table Trim® *(John Morrell & Co.)*

Pea Pod-Cucumber Salad *(bottom)*, Dynasty Beef on Green Cabbage *(top)*
La Choy® *(La Choy Food Products)*

Chinese-Style Pineapple Duckling
(National Duckling Council)

Sukiyaki
A.1. *(Heublein Inc.)*

Chinese Meatballs with Veg-All® Mixed Vegetables
Veg-All® *(The Larsen Company)*

Saucy Spareribs *(right)*, Jolly Shrimp Toast *(left)*
Lipton® *(Thomas J. Lipton, Inc.)*

Stir-Fry Pork with Vegetables
(National Pork Producers Council)

Tangy Pork Kabobs
John Morrell® Table Trim® *(John Morrell & Co.)*

Crabmeat Oriental
(National Marine Fisheries Service)

Mandarin Tuna and Cashews
Chicken of the Sea® *(Ralston Purina Co.)*

Sweet & Sour Pork
Dole® *(Castle & Cooke Foods)*

Shrimp Oriental
ReaLemon® *(Borden Inc.)*

Teriyaki Turkey Wings
Louis Rich™ *(Louis Rich Co., Div. of Oscar Mayer Foods Corp.)*

Shrimp with Snow Peas
(Florida Department of Natural Resources)

True Cod Kabobs, Teriyaki
(National Marine Fisheries Service)

Sweet Sour Pork
Del Monte *(Del Monte Corporation)*

Oriental Turkey Stir-Fry
Louis Rich™ *(Louis Rich Co., Div. of Oscar Mayer Foods Corp.)*

Peking Cornish Hens with Scallion Sauce
Perdue® *(Perdue Farms Inc.)*

Chicken Oriental
Lipton® *(Thomas J. Lipton, Inc.)*

Cantonese Pork Chops
(California Apricot Advisory Board)

Chicken Cashew *(bottom)*, Saucy Stir-Fried Shrimp *(top)*
Wyler's® *(Borden Inc.)*

Chinese Pepper Steak
Coca-Cola® *(The Coca-Cola Company)*

Jade Chicken
Argo®/Kingsford's®, Mazola® *(Best Foods)*

Tempura
Bisquick® *(General Mills, Inc.)*

Ginger Chicken with Peanuts
Birds Eye® *(General Foods)*

Stir Fry Bean Sprouts and Peppers *(left)*, Chinese Vegetable Soup *(right)*, Chicken with Broccoli and Walnuts *(front)*
La Choy® *(La Choy Food Products)*

Polynesian Turkey and Noodles
Mueller's® *(C. F. Mueller Company)*

Beef Sukiyaki in Wok
Diet Shasta® *(Shasta Beverages)*

Sweet and Sour Pork with Cranberries
Ocean Spray® *(Ocean Spray Cranberries, Inc.)*

Kiwifruit Teriyaki Pork
Calavo® *(Calavo Growers of California)*

Penang Pork Chops
French's® *(R. T. French Co.)*

Pepper Steak
Baltimore Spice Old Bay *(The Baltimore Spice Company)*

Teriyaki Burgers
Rice Chex® *(Ralston Purina Co.)*

Sweet-Sour Glazed Cornish
Tyson® *(Tyson Foods, Inc.)*

46

Marinated Beef Strips *(back)*, Chinese Tuna *(front)*
Karo®, Argo®/Kingsford's® *(Best Foods)*

Chinese Chicken with Cherries *(front)*, Cantonese Flank
Steak *(back)*
Stokely's® *(Stokely-Van Camp, Inc.)*

Pork Chow Mein
Wilson® *(Wilson Foods Corp.)*

Stir-Fry Beef and Green Beans
Mazola®, Argo®/Kingsford's® *(Best Foods)*

47

Pacific Isles Rice *(right)*, South Seas Pork
Tidbits *(left)*
Lipton® *(Thomas J. Lipton, Inc.)*

Fluffy Fruit Pie
(American Dry Milk Institute, Inc.)

Almond Cloud
Celestial Seasonings® *(Celestial
Seasonings, Inc.)*

Steamed Almond Snow Cake *(top)*, Chinese Almond Cookies *(right)*, Almond Won Ton
Cookies *(left)* *(Almond Board of California)*

Rock Lobster Foo Yung
(Chinese Rock Lobster Omelets)

16 oz. frozen **SOUTH AFRICAN ROCK LOBSTER Tails**
6 eggs
2 tablespoons soy sauce
½ teaspoon salt
1 can (1 lb.) Chinese vegetables, drained and coarsely chopped
¼ cup chopped scallions
Peanut oil
¼ cup margarine or butter
1 clove garlic, minced
2 tablespoons corn starch
1 can (10½ oz.) condensed beef broth
¾ cup water

Parboil frozen rock lobster tails by dropping them into boiling salted water and cook only until water reboils—just enough to parboil the tails and facilitate removal from shell. Drain immediately, drench with cold water and cut away underside membrane with kitchen shears and pull out meat in one piece. Chop rock lobster meat coarsely. Beat eggs in a bowl with soy sauce, salt. Stir in rock lobster meat, Chinese vegetables, scallions. On a griddle or in a skillet heat about 2 tablespoons oil. Add ¼ cup of the rock lobster mixture and fry until brown on one side. With a pancake turner, turn and brown on the other side. Repeat using remaining mixture adding more oil each time. Keep omelets warm in a 200° F. oven. In a saucepan heat margarine and sauté garlic until golden. Stir in corn starch. Gradually stir in beef broth and water. Stir over low heat until sauce bubbles and thickens. Serve omelets with sauce spooned over them. Serve with white rice and additional soy sauce. *Yield: 6 servings*

Favorite recipe from **South African Rock Lobster Service Corp.**

Japanese Steamed Rock Lobster

3 pkgs. (8 oz. ea.) frozen **SOUTH AFRICAN ROCK LOBSTER Tails**
6 mushrooms, cut into slices
6 scallions, cut into long thin strips
1 cup thinly sliced celery
1 bunch broccoli, trimmed and cut into flowerets
1 tablespoon soy sauce
1 envelope dehydrated chicken broth
¼ cup water

With scissors remove thin underside membrane. Push a bamboo skewer lengthwise through tail to prevent curling. Place a colander over boiling water in a large pot, or use a steamer. Put rock lobster tails into colander and place vegetables on top and around tails. Mix soy sauce, broth and water and brush over tails and vegetables. Cover pot and let steam for 20 minutes or until vegetables

are tender-crisp and tail meat has lost its translucency and is opaque. Serve with fried rice. *Yield: 6 servings*

Favorite recipe from **South African Rock Lobster Service Corp.**

Snow Crab Oriental

1 (6 oz.) can **PACIFIC PEARL** Snow Crab
3 Tbsp. salad oil
1 cup sliced celery
1 (6 oz.) package frozen Chinese pea pods
½ cup sliced onions
½ cup sliced mushrooms
1 (8 oz.) can water chestnuts, drained and sliced
½ cup bean sprouts
⅓ cup toasted almonds, sliced
Hot, cooked rice
Teriyaki sauce

Drain crab meat, flake and cut large pieces into chunks. Heat salad oil in large skillet or wok. Add celery, pea pods, onion and mushrooms; cook until tender-crisp, stirring frequently. Add more oil if necessary. Add crab meat, water chestnuts, bean sprouts and almonds and cook until heated through. To make sauce combine ¼ cup soy sauce, ¼ cup dry white wine, 1 Tbsp. sugar, 1 tsp. cornstarch, ¼ tsp. powdered ginger and ⅛ tsp. garlic powder in small saucepan. Bring to a simmer, then add ¼ cup of sauce to crab mixture. Toss lightly. Serve with hot, cooked rice and rest of sauce. *Makes approximately 5-6 servings*

Crabmeat Oriental

12 ounces blue crabmeat or other crabmeat, fresh, frozen, or pasteurized
1 package (9 ounces) frozen cut green beans, thawed or ½ pound fresh green beans
1 cup coarsely shredded carrot
6 eggs, beaten
¼ teaspoon garlic salt
⅛ teaspoon pepper
Oriental Sauce*

Thaw frozen crabmeat. Drain crabmeat. Remove any remaining shell or cartilage. Cut green beans into ⅛ inch thick diagonal slices. Combine all ingredients. Pour ¼ cup crab mixture into hot greased fry pan. Fry at moderate heat for 2 to 3 minutes or until lightly browned. Turn carefully and fry 2 to 3 minutes longer or until brown. Remove to heated serving platter and keep warm. Repeat until all patties are cooked. Serve with Oriental Sauce. *Makes 6-8 servings, 2 patties each*

*Oriental Sauce

1 tablespoon cornstarch
1 tablespoon soy sauce
2 teaspoons sugar
2 teaspoons cider vinegar
1½ cups chicken broth

In a small saucepan, combine cornstarch, soy sauce, sugar, and vinegar. Add broth gradually and cook until thickened, stirring constantly. *Makes approximately 1½ cups sauce*

CALORIES	167.0	FAT - TOTAL (gms)	7.0
PROTEIN (gms)	18.0	CHOLESTEROL (mgs)	268.0
CARBOHYDRATE (gms)	8.0	SODIUM (mgs)	489.0

Favorite recipe from **National Marine Fisheries Service**

Almond Crab Casserole

1 (6 oz.) pkg. **WAKEFIELD®** Crabmeat
1 can condensed cream of mushroom soup
1 cup chopped celery
¼ cup chopped onion
1 (3 oz.) can chow mein noodles
1 (8 oz.) can water chestnuts, drained and sliced
⅓ cup toasted, slivered almonds
1 (4 oz.) can mushroom pieces
1 teaspoon Worcestershire sauce

Thaw and drain crabmeat and retain liquid. Stir together soup, celery, onion, noodles, water chestnuts, mushrooms and Worcestershire sauce. Fold in crabmeat and crab liquid. Spoon into greased 1½ quart casserole dish. Top with almonds and bake in 350° F. oven for 20-30 minutes or until hot and lightly browned.

Cantonese Shrimp and Beans

1½ pounds frozen raw, peeled, deveined shrimp
1½ teaspoons chicken stock base
1 cup boiling water
¼ cup thinly sliced green onion
1 clove garlic, crushed
1 tablespoon salad oil
1 teaspoon salt
½ teaspoon ginger
Dash pepper
1 package (9 ounces) frozen cut green beans
1 tablespoon cornstarch
1 tablespoon cold water

Thaw frozen shrimp. Dissolve chicken stock base in boiling water. Cook onion, garlic, and shrimp in oil for 3 minutes, stirring frequently. If necessary, add a little of the chicken broth to prevent sticking. Stir in salt, ginger, pepper, green beans, and chicken broth. Cover and simmer 5 to 7 minutes longer or until beans are cooked but still slightly crisp. Combine cornstarch and water. Add cornstarch mixture to shrimp and cook until thick and clear, stirring constantly. *Serves 6*

Calories: Approximately 130 calories in each serving.

Favorite recipe from **National Marine Fisheries Service**

Shrimp with Snow Peas

1 pound shrimp
1 cup water
½ cup chicken broth
¼ cup soy sauce
3 Tablespoons dry sherry or white wine
2 Tablespoons cornstarch
2 teaspoons minced fresh ginger
¼ cup oil
1 6-oz. package frozen snow peas, thawed and patted dry, or ½ lb. fresh snow peas
3 green onions cut in 1 in. pieces
½ can (8-oz.) water chestnuts, sliced

Peel shrimp and if large, split in half lengthways. Combine water, chicken broth, soy sauce, sherry or wine, cornstarch and ginger and set aside. Heat oil hot. Cook the shrimp, snow peas, onions and water chestnuts by adding each separately to the pan or wok over high heat and stirring rapidly for 3 to 4 minutes. When one is finished, remove from the pan or wok, set it aside and put in another ingredient. Cook the shrimp only until they are pink and the vegetables until they are hot and become soft. Put all ingredients back into the pan or wok, stir and add the soy sauce mixture and cook until the sauce thickens slightly, about 2 to 3 minutes. Serve over hot rice. *Makes 4 servings*

Favorite recipe from **Florida Department of Natural Resources**

ReaLemon®
Shrimp Oriental

¼ cup margarine or butter
2 cups sliced fresh mushrooms (about 8 ounces)
1 cup sliced celery
½ cup finely chopped onion
8 ounces raw shrimp, peeled and deveined
⅓ cup **REALEMON®** Lemon Juice from Concentrate
2 tablespoons brown sugar
1 tablespoon soy sauce
¼ teaspoon ground ginger
1 tablespoon cornstarch
¼ cup water
1 (6 ounce) package frozen pea pods, thawed
Hot cooked rice

In large skillet, melt margarine. Add mushrooms, celery and onion; cook until onion is transparent. Stir in shrimp; cook about 3 minutes. Combine **REALEMON®**, sugar, soy sauce and ginger; stir into shrimp mixture. Blend cornstarch with water; gradually stir into shrimp mixture. Add pea pods; bring to a boil. Cook and stir about 1 minute. Serve over rice with additional soy sauce if desired. Refrigerate leftovers. *Makes 4 servings*

Boggs Stir Fry Shrimp

1 lb. raw, shelled large shrimp, cut in half lengthwise
4 teaspoons cornstarch
½ teaspoon ground ginger
1 medium clove garlic, finely minced
⅛ teaspoon salt
2 teaspoons soy sauce
¼ cup chicken broth
¼ cup **BOGGS Cranberry Liqueur**
⅛ teaspoon pepper
3 tablespoons oil
1½ cups broccoli flowerets
1 small onion, chopped
½ cup chopped unsalted cashews

In medium bowl, toss shrimp with 2 teaspoons cornstarch, ginger, garlic and salt. Set aside. In small bowl, combine remaining 2 teaspoons cornstarch, soy sauce, chicken broth, **BOGGS**, and pepper. Set aside. In wok or medium skillet, heat 2 tablespoons oil. Add shrimp. Stirring constantly, cook 1-2 minutes, or until shrimp turn pink. Remove to heated platter. Add remaining 1 tablespoon oil to skillet. Add broccoli and onion. Stirring constantly, cook 1 minute. Add sauce mixture. Cook until slightly thickened. Stir in shrimp. Sprinkle with cashews. Serve immediately. *Serves 4-6*

Wyler's®
Saucy Stir-Fried Shrimp

1 pound medium or large shrimp, peeled, leaving tails
  on and deveined
1 cup thinly sliced carrots
1 clove garlic, finely chopped
2 cups sliced bok choy
1½ cups fresh cauliflowerets
4 ounces fresh bean sprouts *or* 1 (14-ounce) can bean
  sprouts, drained
1 cup sliced fresh mushrooms (about 4 ounces)
4 ounces fresh pea pods *or* 1 (6-ounce) package frozen
  pea pods, thawed
1 tablespoon **WYLER'S® Chicken-Flavor Instant
  Bouillon** *or* **3 Chicken-Flavor Bouillon Cubes**
1¾ cups water
3 tablespoons cornstarch
3 tablespoons soy sauce
1 teaspoon ground ginger
½ teaspoon sugar
3 tablespoons vegetable oil
Hot cooked rice

Prepare shrimp and vegetables. In small saucepan, dissolve bouillon in *1 cup* water. Stir together remaining water, cornstarch, soy sauce, ginger and sugar. Stir into bouillon liquid; set aside. In large skillet or wok, over high heat, cook and stir carrots and garlic in *2 tablespoons* oil 30 seconds. Add remaining vegetables, cook and stir 2 minutes or until vegetables are tender-crisp. Remove vegetables. Add remaining oil; cook and stir shrimp 1 minute. Add vegetables; pour bouillon mixture evenly over top. Cook and stir until thickened and heated through, about 1 minute. Serve immediately with rice. Refrigerate leftovers.

Makes 4 to 6 servings

Shrimp in Lobster and Plum Sauce

A. Have ready:
   ¼ lb. ground lean pork
   ¾ lb. shelled and cleaned medium-size shrimp
   2 scallions, including green part, cut in ⅛ inch rounds
   2 cloves of garlic, minced
B. Mix chow sauce in a bowl:
   1 lightly beaten egg
   3 Tbsp. **CHINA BOWL® Plum Sauce**
   2 Tbsp. **CHINA BOWL® Chinese Light Soy Sauce**
   1 Tbsp. **CHINA BOWL® Chinese Cooking Wine** or
     dry sherry
   1 tsp. sugar
   1 tsp. corn starch in 2 Tbsp. water
C. Cooking: Add 2 Tbsp. peanut or vegetable oil to a wok or large skillet over high heat and, as oil starts to smoke, add shrimp, pork, scallions and garlic and stir fry for 2 minutes. Stir chow sauce, add to wok, reduce flame to medium and stir fry for 2 minutes more. Serves 4 when included in a Chinese family-style meal of 2 other main dishes and rice.

Stir Fried Shrimp and Vegetables

Stir fry 1 pound of any frozen oriental style vegetable mix in 2 tablespoons of hot oil. Cook for 2 minutes. Add 6 ounces thawed **BRILLIANT Cooked Shrimp** and heat 1 additional minute. Serve with white or fried rice. Serve with duck sauce, soy sauce and sharp mustard.

Serves 3-4

Sweet and Pungent Shrimp

Heat ¾ cup duck sauce, 1 tablespoon soy sauce, ½ teaspoon hot sauce to boiling. Toss in 6 ounces thawed **BRILLIANT Cooked Shrimp**. Heat one minute and serve on white or fried rice with mixed salad.

Serves 3

Sweet 'n Pungent Florida Shrimp

2 lb. Florida shrimp, peeled and deveined
1 cup cream of coconut
1 cup pineapple juice
1 cup cider vinegar
¼ cup soy sauce
¼ cup brown sugar (optional)
1 cup Florida orange juice
6 tablespoons cornstarch
2 green peppers, cut into strips
2 tomatoes, cut into thin wedges
8 pitted black olives, sliced
6 Florida oranges, peeled and sectioned
Wild rice with toasted almonds

Poach shrimp until just underdone. Set aside. In a saucepan, mix together cream of coconut, pineapple juice, vinegar, soy sauce and brown sugar (if desired), and bring to a boil. Mix orange juice and cornstarch until smooth; add slowly to coconut mixture, stirring constantly, until mixture boils and thickens. Add green pepper and simmer 5 minutes. Stir in tomatoes and shrimp and simmer another 2 minutes. Toss in olive slices and orange sections and spoon into a serving bowl. Serve with wild rice tossed with toasted almonds.

Yield: 8 servings

Favorite recipe from **State of Florida, Department of Citrus**

Speedy Shrimp Oriental

1 pound **BOOTH® Tender Young Shrimp,** frozen
2 10-oz. packages frozen Chinese vegetables

Cook shrimp according to package directions; drain. In large saucepan cook vegetables as directed on the package. Add cooked shrimp to vegetables and heat through. Serve over rice or Chinese noodles.

Sweet 'N Sour Shrimp

¼ cup thinly sliced onion
1 medium-size green pepper, seeded and cut into strips
2 teaspoons vegetable oil
¼ cup rice vinegar
1 tablespoon soy sauce
2 teaspoons cornstarch
½ teaspoon ginger
1 can (8 ounces) juice-packed crushed pineapple
1 pound shrimp, cooked, shelled, and deveined
6 packets SWEET 'N LOW®

In large non-stick skillet or wok, sauté onion and green pepper in oil until onion is transparent. In separate bowl, mix together vinegar, soy sauce, cornstarch, and ginger. Stir in pineapple and add to skillet. Stir over low heat until mixture thickens. Stir in shrimp and **SWEET 'N LOW®**. Heat thoroughly. Serve over hot cooked rice.   *4 servings*

PER SERVING (1¼ cups): Calories: 170 Protein: 23gm
Carbohydrate: 12gm   Fat: 3gm   Sodium: 496mg

Heart's Delight Shrimp

1 15½ oz. can pineapple chunks or slices cut up
1 large green pepper
4 tablespoons butter
1 1-pound package **BORDO Whole Imported Dates**
1½ pounds cooked, shelled, deveined shrimp

Sauce:
1 cup pineapple juice
¼ teaspoon dry mustard
½ teaspoon ground ginger
¼ cup brown sugar
1 tablespoon cornstarch

Top:
2 tablespoons butter
½ cup dry bread crumbs

Drain pineapple, reserve liquid for sauce. Seed green pepper and slice into ¼ inch strips. Melt butter in large skillet. Sauté green pepper until it just begins to soften, about 2 minutes. Add pineapple chunks and dates and heat through, carefully mixing. Remove mixture from pan with slotted spoon and place in large bowl. Place shrimp in skillet and sauté 2-3 minutes. Mix shrimp with date mixture and place in 1½ quart casserole.

SAUCE:
In small saucepan, put 1 cup reserved pineapple juice (add water if necessary to make 1 cup). Add mustard, ginger and brown sugar and mix well. Blend small amount of water with cornstarch to dissolve, add to pineapple juice. Place over medium heat and cook until thick and clear, stirring constantly. Pour mixture over shrimp in casserole.

TOP:
Melt 2 tablespoons butter in skillet. Add bread crumbs and mix until moistened. Sprinkle over shrimp.

Bake at 350° for 25 minutes. Let stand 10 minutes before serving.   *6 generous portions*

Apple-Shrimp Sauté

¼ cup unsweetened pineapple juice
1 tablespoon soy sauce
⅛ teaspoon ground ginger
6 ounces fresh *or* frozen shrimp
1 Golden Delicious apple, cored and sliced
½ cup fresh *or* frozen peas
1 stalk celery, diagonally sliced
1 green onion, diagonally sliced
1 tablespoon cold water
1 teaspoon cornstarch

Combine pineapple juice, soy sauce and ginger; bring to boil. Add shrimp, apples, peas, celery and green onion. Simmer 5 minutes or until thoroughly heated and shrimp is cooked; stir frequently. Combine water and cornstarch; blend into hot juices in pan. Cook and stir until thickened and clear.   *Makes 2 servings*

Calories: 206 calories each

Favorite recipe from **The Apple Growers of Washington State**

Quick Shrimp Chow Mein

1½ cups diagonally-sliced celery
1 cup sliced onions
1 large green pepper, cut in slivers
12 ounces peeled, deveined raw shrimp
2 tablespoons vegetable oil
1 can (16 ounces) fancy mixed Chinese vegetables
1 can (10¾ ounces) condensed cream of chicken soup
3 tablespoons soy sauce
¼ teaspoon pepper
⅓ cup sliced pimientos
3 cups hot cooked **BLUE RIBBON Rice**
1 can (3 ounces) rice noodles *or* chow mein noodles

Sauté celery, onions, green pepper and shrimp in oil until vegetables are tender crisp and shrimp are pink. Add Chinese vegetables, soup, soy sauce, pepper and pimientos. Heat thoroughly. Serve over beds of fluffy **BLUE RIBBON Rice** and sprinkle with noodles.   *Makes 6 servings*

Mrs. Paul's

Peppers & Shrimp

1 package (6 ounces) **MRS. PAUL'S® Fried Shrimp**
1 tablespoon vegetable oil
1 medium green pepper, cut into bite size strips
3 scallions with tops, chopped
1 medium tomato, chopped in small pieces
⅛ teaspoon ginger
¼ teaspoon garlic powder
1 tablespoon soy sauce
¼ cup water
1 tablespoon cornstarch
½ cup chicken broth
2 cups cooked rice

Prepare **MRS. PAUL'S®** Fried Shrimp as directed on package. Sauté green pepper and scallions in vegetable oil for approximately 5 minutes. Add remaining ingredients except cornstarch, chicken broth and rice. Blend cornstarch and chicken broth; add to pan and simmer mixture until thickened. Place cooked shrimp on rice and pour sauce on top.

Serves 4

Atalanta Shrimp Teriyaki

2 lb. **ATALANTA Frozen Shrimp**, raw, shelled, deveined
1 cup pineapple juice
6 Tbsp. soy sauce
½ cup vegetable oil

Marinate shrimp in juice, soy sauce and oil for 20 minutes. Drain and broil shrimps 4 minutes on each side. Serve with rice.

Yield: 6 servings

Snow Peas with Shrimp

1 tablespoon vegetable oil
12 oz. frozen shrimp, thawed
1 cup diagonally sliced celery
1 can (8 oz.) sliced water chestnuts
1 package (6 oz.) frozen Chinese pea pods, partially thawed
1 medium onion, cut in half crosswise then cut in small wedges
1 package (1⅝ oz.) **DURKEE Chop Suey Sauce Mix**
1 cup water

Heat oil in large skillet or wok over high heat. Add shrimp, stir and cook 1 minute. Add vegetables, cover and cook for 2 minutes. Combine sauce mix and water, add to shrimp and vegetables. Bring sauce to a boil, stirring constantly. Serve immediately.

Serves 4 to 6

Seafood and Vegetable Tempura

Fresh shrimp or prawns (21 to 25-count per pound), shelled, deveined and butterflied, leaving tails on
Fish fillets, cut in 1½ x 2-inch pieces
Green peppers, cut in 1½ x 2-inch pieces
Celery, cut in ½ x 2-inch pieces
Sweet potatoes or carrots, peeled and sliced diagonally in ¼-inch thick slices
Eggplant or zucchini, unpeeled and sliced in ¼-inch thick slices
Large fresh mushrooms, sliced in ¼-inch thick slices
Batter*
Tempura Dipping Sauce**

Drain seafoods and vegetables thoroughly on paper towels; arrange on large platter. Pour vegetable oil for frying at least 4 inches deep into electric frying pan, electric wok or deep, wide frying pan; heat to 375°.

(Continued)

*Batter

1 large-size egg
1¼ cups ice-cold water
2 cups sifted cake flour

Beat egg thoroughly with wire wisk or hand rotary beater (not electric). Blend in water. Sprinkle all of flour evenly over liquid. With same wire wisk or beater, stir in flour quickly only until flour is moistened and large lumps disappear. Batter should be very lumpy. Do not stir batter after it is mixed. To fry shrimp, hold one at a time by the tail and dip into batter. Drain off excess batter slightly and slide shrimp gently into hot oil. Repeat with 3 or 4 more shrimp. Fry shrimp about 1 minute, turn over and fry 1 minute longer, or until lightly golden brown. Dip and fry other ingredients in same manner as shrimp. Drain tempura on paper towels or on wire rack over cake pan. Skim off pieces of cooked batter from oil with wire strainer.

**Tempura Dipping Sauce

1½ cups hot water
½ cup **KIKKOMAN** Soy Sauce
¼ teaspoon grated fresh ginger root
⅛ teaspoon monosodium glutamate

Combine all ingredients and pour into small individual bowls. Serve with tempura.

Makes about 6 servings

Oyster Beef Rice

1 can (8 oz.) **BUMBLE BEE®** Whole Oysters
1 pound boneless chuck steak
1 tablespoon diced gingerroot
2 tablespoons oil
¾ cup water
2 tablespoons soy sauce
1 tablespoon cornstarch
4 stalks green onion, cut in 2-inch strips
Hot fluffy rice

Drain oysters, reserving liquid. Cut steak into thin strips. Brown steak with gingerroot in oil. Combine reserved oyster liquid, water, soy sauce and cornstarch. Pour into beef and cook until sauce is clear and thickened. Remove from heat. Stir in oysters and onion. Cover and steam to heat through. Serve with hot fluffy rice.

Makes 4 servings

Oyster Tempura

1 can (8 oz.) **BUMBLE BEE®** Whole Oysters
1 small eggplant
1 egg
1 cup ice water
¾ cup flour
1 teaspoon salt
1 teaspoon paprika
⅛ teaspoon baking powder
Oil for frying
3 large zucchini, chunked

Drain oysters. Cut unpared eggplant into bite-size pieces. Beat egg and ice water until frothy. Beat in flour, salt, paprika, and baking powder. Heat 1-inch oil to 375°F on a thermometer. Dip oysters in batter. Fry until golden. Drain on paper towels. Repeat with eggplant and zucchini. Serve immediately with soy sauce.

Makes 4 to 6 servings

Tempura

Vegetable oil
3 cups **BISQUICK® Baking Mix**
1½ cups water
2 eggs
½ pound shelled and deveined fresh shrimp, 1 can (7 ounces) large shrimp, rinsed and drained, or 1 package (8 ounces) frozen shrimp, thawed
½-pound sole fillet, cut into 1½-inch pieces
1 cup pared eggplant strips, 2 x ¼-inch
1 cup parsley sprigs
4 ounces mushrooms, cut into halves
2 carrots, cut into 2 x ¼-inch strips
1 green pepper, cut into 2 x ¼-inch strips
Sauce*
Shredded radish, drained

Heat oil (1 inch) in electric skillet or wok to 350°. Beat baking mix, water and eggs with hand beater until smooth. Pat shrimp, sole and vegetables dry with paper towel. Dip into batter, allowing excess batter to drip into bowl. Fry several pieces at a time in hot oil, turning once, until golden brown, 2 to 3 minutes; drain on paper towel. Dip into Sauce, then into radish.   *6 servings*

*Sauce

Mix ¼ cup soy sauce, ¼ cup white wine vinegar and 1 tablespoon finely chopped green onion.

Note: Tempura can be made ahead. Wrap in aluminum foil and refrigerate or freeze no longer than 24 hours. To reheat: Heat oven to 400°. Place refrigerated or frozen food on ungreased cookie sheet. Heat until hot, refrigerated food about 15 minutes, frozen food about 25 minutes; drain on paper towel.

Poultry

ARGO®/ KINGSFORD'S®
Jade Chicken

2 whole chicken breasts, boned, skinnned, cut into 1-inch pieces
1 tablespoon **ARGO®/KINGSFORD'S® Corn Starch**
3 tablespoons **MAZOLA® Corn Oil,** divided
2 medium green peppers, cut in 1-inch squares (1½ cups)
¼ cup sliced green onion
1 tablespoon minced fresh ginger root
1 clove garlic, minced or pressed
½ cup chicken bouillon
1 tablespoon soy sauce
4 whole cashew nuts, split in half (optional)

In small bowl toss together chicken and corn starch to coat evenly. In large skillet heat 1 tablespoon of the corn oil over medium-high heat. Add green peppers, onion, ginger and garlic; stir-fry 3 minutes or until vegetables are tender-crisp. Remove from skillet. In same pan heat remaining 2 tablespoons corn oil. Add chicken; stir-fry 3 minutes or until chicken turns milky white. Return vegetables to skillet. Add bouillon and soy sauce. Stirring constantly, bring to boil over medium heat and boil 1 minute. Garnish with cashew halves. If desired, serve over rice.

Makes 4 servings

Chinese Chicken with Cherries

2 whole boned, skinned chicken breasts
½ cup sugar
2 Tablespoons cornstarch
2 Tablespoons plus 1 teaspoon lemon juice
2 Tablespoons water
2 Tablespoons vegetable oil, divided
1 package (14 ounces) **Frozen STOKELY'S® Chinese Style Stir-Fry Vegetables**
1 cup **Frozen STOKELY'S® Dark Sweet Cherries,** thawed
Soy sauce

Cut chicken into 1-inch cubes. Combine sugar, cornstarch, lemon juice and water; blend until smooth. Set aside. Heat 9- or 10-inch skillet or wok over high heat (a drop of water will sizzle). Pour 1 Tablespoon oil in wide, circular motion inside rim of pan. Tilt pan to coat surface; add chicken and stir-fry about 1½ minutes, or until chicken turns white. Push chicken to side. Remove seasoning packet from vegetables and reserve; add frozen vegetables to pan. Pour remaining oil around rim of pan quickly. Toss vegetables to coat each piece. Cover and cook 3 minutes, stirring once midway. If vegetables begin to stick, reduce temperature slightly or add 1 teaspoon oil. Sprinkle reserved seasoning packet over mixture and blend. Cook about 30 seconds more. Push vegetables and meat to sides. Give reserved sauce a quick stir and pour into center of pan. When it comes to a boil, stir in vegetables and chicken. Add cherries; stir, remove from heat and serve with soy sauce.

4 servings

Stir-Fried Tofu with Chicken

1 tablespoon whole wheat flour
3 tablespoons natural soy sauce (Tamari)
½ cup vegetable stock or water
1 to 2 tablespoons **HEALTH VALLEY® Best Blend Oil**
1 clove garlic, minced
½ cup chopped onions
1 teaspoon finely minced fresh ginger root
1 double breast and 2 thighs **HEALTH VALLEY® Frozen Cut-Up Chicken,** partially thawed, boned, skinned and cut into ¼-inch strips
1 package **HEALTH VALLEY® Hard Tofu,** cut into 1-inch cubes and drained on paper towels
½ package **HEALTH VALLEY® Frozen Peas** or 1 package **HEALTH VALLEY® Frozen Pea Pods with Water Chestnuts,** thawed but not cooked

In a small bowl, mix flour, soy sauce and stock or water. Set aside. In a wok, heat oil until it is very hot. Add garlic, onions and ginger, and stir-fry for about 1 minute, then add chicken and continue to stir-fry for 10 minutes longer. Stir in flour-soy mixture and continue to stir until thickened. Then add tofu and peas or pea pods, and cook five minutes more. Serve immediately. Total preparation time: 30 minutes.   *Yield: 6 servings*

Chicken with Broccoli and Walnuts

2 raw chicken breasts, boned and cut into 1-inch cubes
1 teaspoon salt
1 teaspoon sugar
3 tablespoons sherry
1 tablespoon **LA CHOY® Soy Sauce**
3 tablespoons cornstarch
1 egg, beaten
½ cup cooking oil
1 cup walnut halves, blanched
2 teaspoons minced fresh ginger root
2 cloves garlic, minced
½ cup boiling water
1 can (8 oz.) **LA CHOY® Bamboo Shoots,** drained
1 pkg. (8 oz.) frozen broccoli, thawed

Combine chicken with salt, sugar, sherry and soy sauce. Let stand 30 minutes. Drain, reserving marinade. Coat chicken with cornstarch and mix in egg.

Heat oil in wok or large skillet; add walnuts and brown. Remove and drain. Pour off all but 2 tablespoons oil. Brown chicken, ginger and garlic. Add water, bamboo shoots and marinade; cover and cook over low heat 15 minutes. Add walnuts and broccoli and cook 2 minutes more.   *4-5 servings*

Chicken and Chinese Peapods

1 frying chicken, boned and cut in small pieces
2 tablespoons cornstarch
2 slices fresh ginger, slivered
1 package **KUBLA KHAN Chinese Peapods**
3 tablespoons oil
¾ teaspoon salt
½ teaspoon monosodium glutamate

Dredge chicken in cornstarch. Sauté ginger in oil on high heat. Sauté chicken in oil. When chicken is done, in about 8 minutes, add Chinese Peapods and seasoning. Sauté for 10 minutes on high heat. Serve at once.   *Serves 4*

Stir-Fry Chicken Fillets with Zucchini

1 12-oz. package **TYSON® CHICK 'N QUICK™
  Breast Fillets** (8-12 pieces)
¼ cup oil
2 cloves crushed garlic
3 Tbsp. soy sauce
½ cup bamboo shoots
½ cup canned mushroom slices
2 cups diced zucchini
2 Tbsp. cornstarch in ½ cup water
Roasted slivered almonds

Stir-fry chicken fillets over high heat with garlic and oil for 3 to 4 minutes. Add soy sauce and continue stirring for several minutes. Add zucchini, mushrooms, and bamboo shoots, cover and cook a few minutes.

Add cornstarch paste and stir for about 1 minute. Garnish with roasted slivered almonds.   *Yield: 4-6 servings*

Chicken Sung

A. Dice into cubes about pine nut size 1 **double chicken breast** (partial freezing aids in slicing). Place cubes in bowl with **1 egg white, 1 Tbsp. corn starch** and ½ **tsp. salt.** Blend with fingers and refrigerate ½ hour or longer.
B. Dice into cubes, as above, these vegetables:
     ¼ cup each of carrot and celery
     6 water chestnuts
     1 scallion, including green leaves
C. Toast ¼ cup **CHINA BOWL® Pine Nuts**
D. Mince:
     2 cloves garlic
     ½-inch round of **CHINA BOWL® Fresh Ginger**
E. Mix chow sauce in a bowl:
     2 Tbsp. **CHINA BOWL® Chili Paste with Garlic** or
     ½ tsp. **CHINA BOWL® Hot Oil** (or to taste)
     2 Tbsp. **CHINA BOWL® Chinese Cooking Wine** or
     dry sherry
     1 Tbsp. **CHINA BOWL® Chinese Light Soy Sauce**
     1 tsp. corn starch
     ¼ tsp. **CHINA BOWL® Taste Powder-MSG**
     (optional)
F. Cooking: Add ¼ cup peanut or vegetable oil to a wok or large skillet over high heat and, as oil starts to smoke, add ginger and garlic and stir fry for 10 seconds. Add chicken mixture and stir fry while separating chicken for 1½ minutes more. Add vegetables and stir fry for 30 seconds more. Stir chow sauce, add to wok, reduce flame to medium and stir fry 2 minutes more. Add ¼ tsp. **CHINA BOWL® Sesame Oil** (optional) and pine nuts, stir briefly and turn mixture onto a heated platter. Serve with whole cold iceberg lettuce leaves, in each of which a heaping Tbsp. of mixture is added and eaten sandwich fashion.

Serves 6 to 8 as an appetizer, and 4 as a main course

Cookin' Good™ Shanghai

2 pounds of **COOKIN' GOOD™ Chicken Breasts,**
  skinned, boned and cut in thin strips
¼ cup peanut or other vegetable oil
1 cup celery cut on the bias—½ inch pieces
1 cup slivered green onions
1 can or 1 pound of fresh beansprouts
1 can (5 oz.) water chestnuts, drained and sliced thin
¼ pound sliced fresh mushrooms
¼ cup slivered, toasted almonds
1 clove of garlic, minced or pressed
¼ cup soy sauce
¼ cup sherry or water
1 tablespoon cornstarch
1 teaspoon minced fresh ginger or
  ¼ teaspoon of powdered ginger

Combine sherry, soy sauce, and cornstarch; set aside. Heat the oil in a wok or heavy skillet. Add chicken and stir-fry until chicken turns white, approximately 3-4 minutes. Add the celery, green onions, mushrooms, garlic and ginger, and cook 2 minutes. Pour in the liquid, add beansprouts and water chestnuts; stir-cook three minutes. Serve over rice and garnish with almonds.

Teriyaki Sesame Fried Chicken

1 package (2 lb.) BANQUET® Heat and Serve
   Frozen Fully Cooked Fried Chicken
2 tablespoons teriyaki sauce
1 tablespoon sesame seeds

Place chicken on shallow baking pan. Brush with teriyaki sauce.
Sprinkle sesame seeds on top. Heat in 375°F oven 30 to 35 minutes
or until hot.
Makes 5 servings

Orange Teriyaki Chicken

2 broiler-fryer chickens, (2½ pounds each, quartered)
1 can (6 ounces) frozen concentrated orange juice
   thawed and undiluted
¼ cup soy sauce
2 tablespoons chopped onion
1 tablespoon vegetable oil
2 teaspoons AC'CENT® Flavor Enhancer
½ teaspoon ground ginger
½ teaspoon hot pepper sauce

Combine concentrated orange juice, soy sauce, onion, oil,
AC'CENT®, ginger, and hot pepper sauce. Marinate chicken at
least 3 hours, refrigerated, turning once. Broil 40 minutes or grill
slowly, 6 to 8 inches away from source of heat 30 to 45 minutes.
Turn chicken several times during cooking, brushing frequently
with remaining marinade.
Yield: 6 servings

Easy Vegetable and Chicken Sushi

4 cups cooked rice
¼ cup MARUKAN® Seasoned Gourmet Rice Vinegar
1 carrot
5 mushrooms
12 string beans
1 split chicken breast (1 cup pork may be used instead)
3 Tbsp. soy sauce
1 tsp. sugar
1 Tbsp. cooking oil
1 tsp. monosodium glutamate

After rice is cooked, mix gently with wooden paddle and ladle into
a large bowl. Cool rice. Pour vinegar over the cooled rice and fluff
lightly to mix. Slice carrots, string beans very thin diagonally.
Slice mushrooms. Debone and slice chicken into small thin slices.
Add oil to a pan and sauté chicken. Add carrots and green beans.
Cook about 10 minutes or until barely tender. Add mushrooms and
cook about 2 minutes more. Season with sugar, soy sauce and
monosodium glutamate. Cool and mix lightly with rice until ingredients are evenly distributed.

Durkee®

Low Salt Oriental Chicken

¼ cup flour
2 tablespoons sugar
2 tablespoons DURKEE Ground Mustard
½ teaspoon DURKEE Garlic Powder
¼ teaspoon DURKEE Ground Ginger
¼ teaspoon DURKEE Ground Turmeric
1½ cups cold water
3 tablespoons molasses
1 tablespoon lemon juice
2 chicken breasts (about 2 pounds), skinned, boned
   and sliced in strips
2 tablespoons vegetable oil
1½ cups sliced celery, cut diagonally
1 medium green pepper, cut in strips
½ cup chopped onion

Combine flour, sugar, and spices. Gradually add cold water,
mixing thoroughly. Add molasses and lemon juice. Set aside.
Brown chicken in vegetable oil. Add celery, green pepper and
onion; sauté 5 minutes. Pour flour mixture over chicken, stirring
constantly. Simmer, covered, 30 minutes. Serve over rice.
Makes 4 to 6 servings

About 64 mg. sodium per 6 servings or 96 mg. sodium per 4 servings.

Chinese Chicken and Pea Pods

1 lb. boneless chicken, skinned, cut in 1-inch pieces
1 Tbsp. vegetable oil
1 jar LA SAUCE® Chicken Baking Sauce—Chinese
   Style
1 16 oz. can bean sprouts, drained
1 6 oz. package frozen pea pods, partially thawed
Chow mein noodles

In large fry pan, brown chicken in oil on medium heat 5 minutes,
stirring frequently. Stir in LA SAUCE®; simmer, covered, on low
heat 10 minutes, stirring occasionally. Stir in bean sprouts and pea
pods; simmer on medium heat 2 minutes, stirring frequently.
Serve on noodles.
4 servings

Barbecued Chicken Oriental

Make a basting sauce of ½ cup salad oil, ½ cup COLGIN HICK-
ORY LIQUID SMOKE, 1 #2 can tomato juice, ½ cup dry wine,
5 drops liquid pepper seasoning, dash of soy, juice of one lemon,
salt and pepper to taste.
  Brush sauce on the split chicken or chicken breast before cooking. Baste the chicken frequently. Cook well done to a golden
brown. Try this sauce baste for your outdoor charcoal broil.

PREMIUM
Saltine Crackers

Chinese Skillet Dinner

22 PREMIUM Saltine Crackers
2 tablespoons butter or margarine
1 cup diagonally sliced celery
¼ cup sliced scallions
1 (19-ounce) can chunky chicken with rice soup
2 cups cubed cooked chicken
1 (10-ounce) package frozen chopped broccoli
2 tablespoons lemon juice
Soy sauce, optional

1.   Finely roll 7 **PREMIUM Saltine Crackers** to yield about ¼ cup crumbs; set aside. Using a sharp serrated knife, thinly slice remaining 15 saltines; set aside.
2.   In large skillet, over medium heat, melt butter or margarine; sauté celery and scallions about 5 minutes, or until tender.
3.   Add soup, chicken, broccoli and lemon juice; over medium heat, bring to a boil. Cover; reduce heat; simmer about 5 minutes, or until broccoli is tender-crisp. Blend in saltine crumbs.
4.   *To Serve*: Spoon into serving bowl; if desired, sprinkle with soy sauce. Arrange sliced saltines in center.

Makes 5 to 6 servings

MICROWAVE METHOD:
Finely roll and thinly slice **PREMIUM Saltine Crackers** as in Step 1. In 3-quart microwave-proof bowl, microwave butter or margarine, celery and scallions 4 minutes, stirring after 2 minutes, until vegetables are tender. Add remaining ingredients, except saltines, and, if desired, soy sauce; cover with plastic wrap. Microwave at 100% power 6 minutes, stirring every 2 minutes, until broccoli is tender-crisp. Blend in saltine crumbs; serve as in Step 4.

Calorie Watcher's Chinese Chicken with Spaghetti

1 (7-ounce) package **CREAMETTE® Italian Style Spaghetti** or **Elbow Macaroni,** cooked as package directs and drained
2 whole chicken breasts (about 1½ pounds) skinned, boned and cut into strips
6 ounces fresh mushrooms, sliced (about 1½ cups)
½ cup chopped green onions
3 tablespoons low calorie margarine
2 cups water
1 tablespoon chicken-flavor instant bouillon
2 teaspoons cornstarch
1 (6-ounce) package frozen pea pods, thawed *or*
   1 (10-ounce) package frozen green peas, thawed
2 tablespoons chopped pimiento
2 tablespoons soy sauce
¼ to ½ teaspoon ground ginger

In large skillet or Dutch oven, cook chicken, mushrooms and onions in margarine until chicken is tender and liquid is absorbed.

Meanwhile, stir together water, bouillon and cornstarch. Add to chicken mixture along with cooked spaghetti and remaining ingredients; mix well. Heat through. Serve with additional soy sauce if desired. Refrigerate leftovers.   *Makes 6 servings*

Prepared as directed, provides approximately 310 calories per serving. (Values by product analyses and recipe calculations.)

Chinese Imperial Chicken

1¼ lb. skinned, boned chicken breasts, cut into 1-inch pieces

Marinade:
2 tablespoons **LA CHOY® Soy Sauce**
1½ teaspoons dry vermouth
1 teaspoon Oriental sesame oil
2 tablespoons cold water
1 tablespoon cornstarch

Spinach mixture:
2 packages (10 oz. each) frozen spinach
1 teaspoon salt
1 teaspoon Oriental sesame oil
1 tablespoon minced garlic

Vegetable mixture:
2 tablespoons chopped green onion
2 tablespoons minced fresh ginger
2 tablespoons minced garlic
3 cans (8 oz. each) **LA CHOY® Water Chestnuts,** drained and halved

Sauce mixture:
2 tablespoons dry vermouth
3 tablespoons **LA CHOY® Soy Sauce**
1½ tablespoons sugar
1½ teaspoons Oriental sesame oil
2½ teaspoons Worcestershire sauce
½ teaspoon hot pepper sauce, or to taste
⅓ cup chicken broth
1 tablespoon cornstarch

Cooking oil
1½ cups roasted cashews (if salted, shake in sieve to remove salt)

Combine all ingredients for marinade and pour over chicken, mixing well. Let stand 20 minutes at room temperature.

Meanwhile, cook spinach according to package directions. Rinse under cold water to stop cooking; drain. Toss with seasonings. Arrange around border of serving platter. Set aside.

Combine vegetable mixture; set aside. Combine sauce mixture; set aside.

In wok or deep saucepan, heat oil for deep frying. Drain chicken pieces; fry a few at a time until golden brown. Drain on paper towels.

In a large skillet or wok placed over medium high heat, heat three tablespoons cooking oil. Add vegetable mixture; cook and stir 1 minute. Add sauce mixture; cook and stir until sauce thickens. Add chicken pieces and cashews; cook and stir 1 or 2 minutes or until chicken is heated through. Spoon into center of service platter. Serve immediately.   *4 servings*

Ginger Chicken with Peanuts

½ to ¾ pound cubed raw chicken
1 tablespoon soy sauce
1 teaspoon cornstarch
2 tablespoons oil
1 package (10 oz.) **BIRDS EYE® Japanese** or
   Chinese Style Vegetables With a Seasoned Sauce
¼ cup water
½ teaspoon ginger
2 tablespoons salted peanuts

Combine chicken and soy sauce in bowl; stir in cornstarch. Sauté chicken in hot oil in skillet until just tender, about 3 or 4 minutes. Remove from pan. Add vegetables, water and ginger to skillet. Bring to a *full* boil over medium heat, separating vegetables with a fork and stirring frequently. Reduce heat; cover and simmer 2 minutes. Add chicken and heat. Sprinkle with peanuts. Serve over hot cooked rice, if desired.   *Makes about 3 cups or 3 servings*

Tropical Almond Chicken with Tangy Orange Sauce

Almond Chicken:
⅔ cup **BLUE DIAMOND® Blanched Slivered Almonds,** toasted
¼ cup shredded coconut
½ teaspoon salt
¼ teaspoon pepper
2 chicken breasts, halved and skinned
1 egg, beaten

Process ½ cup of the almonds in blender or food processor until finely ground (reserve remaining almonds to garnish sauce). Mix together ground almonds, coconut, salt and pepper. Dip chicken pieces in egg then in almond mixture to coat. Place in lightly greased baking dish and bake in 425 degree F oven for 25 to 30 minutes, or until just tender.

Makes 4 servings

Tangy Orange Sauce:
½ cup plain yogurt
2 teaspoons cornstarch
½ cup orange juice
1 tablespoon granulated sugar
1 tablespoon grated orange peel

In small saucepan, mix together yogurt and cornstarch until well blended; add orange juice, sugar and orange peel. Cook over medium heat, stirring occasionally, until mixture boils; reduce heat and simmer 1 minute. Pour into serving dish and sprinkle with reserved almonds. Serve along with Almond Chicken.

Makes about 1 cup sauce

Pineapple Chicken Oriental

½ cup **WISH-BONE® Italian Dressing**
1 can (20 oz.) crushed pineapple, drained (reserve liquid)
3 tablespoons firmly packed brown sugar
½ teaspoon ground ginger
4 whole chicken breasts skinned, boned, and pounded
⅓ cup finely chopped green pepper
⅓ cup slivered almonds
1 tablespoon cornstarch

In shallow baking dish, combine Italian dressing, reserved liquid, sugar, and ginger; mix well. Add chicken and marinate 3 hours in refrigerator, turning occasionally.

Preheat oven to 375°. In small bowl, combine pineapple, green pepper, and almonds. Remove chicken; drain and reserve marinade. Spread ¼ pineapple mixture on each chicken breast; roll up and place seam side down in baking dish. Pour ¼ cup marinade over chicken and bake 35 minutes or until chicken is tender.

Remove chicken to heated platter. In small saucepan, combine cooked and reserved marinades with cornstarch; heat, stirring constantly, until slightly thickened, about 2 minutes. Serve over chicken.

Makes 4 servings

Lemon Chicken Oriental

1 garlic clove, minced
2 tablespoons butter or margarine
4 chicken legs with thighs, separated
2 teaspoons salt
¼ teaspoon pepper
2½ cups chicken broth
1 cup **UNCLE BEN'S® CONVERTED® Brand Rice**
2 tablespoons lemon juice
1 small sweet red or green pepper, cut into julienne strips
⅓ cup sliced green onions with tops
1 tablespoon soy sauce
1 package (10 oz.) frozen broccoli spears, partially thawed
1 tablespoon cornstarch
½ cup cold water

Sauté garlic in butter in 10-inch skillet 2 to 3 minutes. Season chicken with 1 teaspoon of the salt and the pepper. Add chicken to skillet; brown on all sides over medium heat. Reduce heat; cover and cook until chicken is tender, about 25 minutes. While chicken is cooking, bring chicken broth to a boil in medium saucepan. Add rice, 1 tablespoon of the lemon juice and remaining 1 teaspoon salt. Cover and simmer 20 minutes. Remove from heat. Stir in red pepper and green onions; let stand covered until all liquid is absorbed, about 5 minutes. When chicken is tender, remove and keep warm; pour off all but 1 tablespoon fat. Add soy sauce and the remaining 1 tablespoon lemon juice to drippings. Add chicken and broccoli to skillet. Cover and simmer 5 minutes. Spoon rice onto serving platter; arrange chicken and broccoli on rice. Combine cornstarch and water; stir into pan drippings. Cook and stir until thickened. Pour sauce over chicken, broccoli and rice.

Makes 4 to 6 servings

Chicken Lettuce Bundles

1 whole chicken breast, about 1 pound, split
½ cup **SMUCKER'S Low Sugar Orange Marmalade**
½ cup cooked rice
¼ cup chopped green onions
4 teaspoons soy sauce
⅛ teaspoon crushed red pepper
1 large head iceberg lettuce
Large green onion tops (about 8 inches long)

Place chicken, skin-side down, on broiler rack over a pan. Broil about 4 inches from heat source for 20 minutes; turn and continue to broil until chicken is fork tender. Cool chicken; remove skin and bones. Pull chicken meat into shreds and place in a bowl. Add Orange Marmalade, rice, chopped onions, soy sauce and pepper. Chill.

Remove core from lettuce. Separate lettuce into individual leaves. Using tongs, dip each leaf into a large saucepan of boiling water just until wilted. Drain well on paper towels. Cut out the coarse, heavy stems at the base of the lettuce leaves.

Dip green onion tops into boiling water just to wilt. Drain and pat dry. Cut onion tops lengthwise into ⅛-inch wide strips to use like string to tie the bundles.

For each lettuce bundle, cut a lettuce leaf into about a 4½-inch square. (You may need to piece some leaves together to form a square.) Place ½ tablespoon of chicken filling diagonally across the lettuce leaf. Bring one corner up over filling; bring two opposite ends toward center to enclose filling and roll up to form an envelope-like package. Tie with a green onion string across the center of each package. Continue stuffing lettuce leaves until the filling has been used.

Arrange on plate and refrigerate until serving time. If prepared ahead, drain off any moisture that accumulates in plate before serving.

Makes about 2½ dozen

Sweet and Salty Chinese Chicken

3 tablespoons butter or margarine
3 scallions, chopped, including greens
½ teaspoon ground ginger
4 each chicken drumsticks, thighs and wings
½ cup soy sauce
½ cup honey
⅓ cup **HOLLAND HOUSE® Sherry Cooking Wine**
2 cups water

Melt butter or margarine in large skillet or frying pan. Add scallions and ginger, then add chicken pieces and brown lightly on both sides. In a small mixing bowl, blend remaining ingredients. Add to chicken and bring to boil. Reduce heat, cover, and simmer for 1 hour 40 minutes. Turn every 25 minutes. Uncover, increase heat and cook another 15 minutes, or until broth is thickened and coats chicken. Serve hot or cold.

Serves 4 to 6

Chicken Cantonese

2 pounds choice chicken pieces
1 teaspoon *each* garlic salt and paprika
¼ teaspoon ground black pepper
2 tablespoons vegetable oil
1 large onion, sliced
1½ large green peppers, cut in thin strips
1 cup diagonally sliced celery
1¼ cups chicken broth, divided
2 tablespoons cornstarch
3 tablespoons soy sauce
2 large fresh tomatoes, cut in eighths
3 cups hot cooked **DORE® Rice**

Remove skin and bones from chicken. Cut meat in thin strips. Sprinkle with seasonings. Sauté chicken in oil 1 to 2 minutes. Add onion, green peppers, celery, and ½ cup broth. Cover; steam 2 minutes. Blend remaining broth with cornstarch and soy sauce. Stir into chicken mixture. Add tomatoes; cook and stir 2 minutes or until sauce is slightly thickened. Serve over beds of fluffy rice.

Makes 6 servings

Oriental Walnut Chicken

¼ cup soy sauce
½ cup white wine
2 teaspoons sugar
½ teaspoon ground ginger
¼ cup sliced green onions
1 package (2 lb.) **BANQUET® Heat and Serve Frozen Fully Cooked Fried Chicken**
¾ cup (3 oz.) walnut pieces

In small bowl, combine soy sauce, wine, sugar, ginger, and onions. Place chicken in 2-quart oblong baking dish. Top with walnuts. Spoon wine mixture evenly over chicken pieces. Heat in 375°F oven 35 to 40 minutes or until hot.   *Makes 5 servings*

Mandarin Orange Chicken

3 pound frying chicken, cut into serving pieces
4 **CELESTIAL SEASONINGS® Mandarin Orange Spice™ Tea Bags**
½ cup boiling water
½ cup soy sauce
2 Tbsp. honey
2 tsp. vegetable oil

Open tea bags and empty contents into a bowl. Add the boiling water and let stand about 5 minutes. Stir in honey, soy sauce and oil.

Put chicken in a glass baking dish. Pour marinade over chicken. Cover and allow to marinate for 3-4 hours at room temperature, turning once. (Can be marinated overnight in the refrigerator.)

Bake chicken in marinade (covered) at 325° for an hour or until chicken is tender. Serve marinade over rice.

East-West Chicken Drumsticks

(Microwave Recipe)

2 pounds COUNTRY PRIDE® Broiler-Fryer Chicken Drumsticks
1 cup corn flake crumbs
1 teaspoon salt
⅛ teaspoon pepper
½ cup evaporated milk
1 tablespoon soy sauce
Mustard sauce*

Mix corn flake crumbs with salt and pepper in shallow dish. Mix evaporated milk and soy sauce in another shallow dish. Dip chicken drumsticks in evaporated milk, then roll immediately in seasoned corn flake crumbs. Place drumsticks in lightly greased 12 x 7½ x 2-inch glass baking dish. Cover with waxed paper and cook in microwave oven 10 minutes, turn dish, cook 8 to 10 minutes longer. Let stand 3 to 5 minutes. Serve with Mustard Sauce if desired. Total cooking time: 20 minutes.   *Yield: 4 to 6 servings*

*Mustard Sauce

¼ cup prepared mustard
1 teaspoon sugar
½ teaspoon salt
⅛ teaspoon TABASCO® Pepper Sauce
½ cup evaporated milk
1 teaspoon lemon juice

In small glass bowl or 2-cup glass measuring cup mix all ingredients except lemon juice. Cover with waxed paper and cook in microwave oven 2 minutes. Stir in lemon juice. Serve with chicken drumsticks. Cooking time: 2 minutes.   *Yield: ¾ cup*

Note: 2 pounds COUNTRY PRIDE® Chicken Wings may be substituted for drumsticks.

Chicken Chow Mein Casserole

3 Tbsp. butter or margarine
⅓ cup chopped onion
¼ cup chopped green pepper
½ cup mushrooms
¼ cup flour
1 can CHINA BEAUTY® Chicken Chop Suey or Chow Mein
1 cup milk
1¼ tsp. CHINA BEAUTY® Soy Sauce
1 chopped hard boiled egg
2 cups cooked plain noodles
1 can crushed CHINA BEAUTY® Chow Mein Noodles

Make a sauce by heating the butter or margarine in pan, add onion and pepper, cooking until onion browns. Add mushrooms and cook several minutes. Blend in flour, add milk, soy sauce, hard

boiled egg, and heat until thoroughly blended. In a greased casserole, layer the cooked noodles, Chicken Chop Suey or Chow Mein, the sauce, making two layers of each. Cover with crushed Chow Mein Noodles. Bake in a moderate oven, 350° F., for 30-35 minutes.   *Serves 8*

Delicious Chicken Coconut

(Ono moa niu)

1 fryer & 2 chicken breasts
6 Tbsp. butter
½ cup flour
1 cup heavy cream
2 cups hot chicken broth
3 tsp. salt
1 tsp. monosodium glutamate
1 13½ oz. can pineapple tidbits
3 large fresh CALAVO® Coconuts

Cook chicken in water. Bone meat, sprinkle with 1 tsp. of salt. Strain, measure 2 cups broth. Melt butter, add flour, hot cream, and chicken broth to make medium thick sauce. Season with 2 tsp. salt and monosodium glutamate. Fold in chicken pieces and pineapple tidbits. Use saw to cut off each end of coconut for a standing surface. Saw nuts in half. Drain milk once cut is made. Rinse shells. Fill coconut halves with chicken mixture. Cover each with foil. Place shells in ½ inch water in baking pan. Bake in 350° oven for 45 minutes. Remove foil last 5 minutes. Serve with grapefruit spoons so coconut meat can be eaten with chicken.
Serves 6

Japanese Chicken Sukiyaki

2½ to 3 lb. uncooked chicken
3 Tbsp. shortening
1 large onion, sliced
1 can bamboo shoots, sliced
¼ cup sugar
¾ cup soy sauce
¾ cup hot water and mushroom liquid
1 can mushrooms
1 lb. watercress, sliced
5 green onions, sliced (tops included)
2 tsp. GRAVY MASTER

Cut chicken from bones and fry in hot shortening. Add onion and bamboo shoots. (The latter can be purchased at a specialty shop.) Add 3 tablespoons sugar, ¼ cup soy sauce, and ½ cup liquid. Boil gently for 5 minutes. Add mushrooms, watercress, and green onions. Continue cooking, adding remaining sugar, soy sauce, GRAVY MASTER and liquid, a little at a time, as needed. Cook a few minutes more.   *Makes six servings*

Carl Buddig

Cantonese Chicken Dish

1 **Family Pak BUDDIG Smoked Sliced Chicken,** cut up
1 package (10 oz.) frozen Chinese style vegetables, cooked and drained
2 cups cooked rice
1 can (10¾ oz.) cream of chicken soup
2 tablespoons sherry
2 tablespoons soy sauce
½ cup chow mein noodles, crushed

CONVENTIONAL METHOD:
Combine all ingredients except chow mein noodles in 1½ quart glass casserole. Stir to mix well. Cover and bake in 350° F. oven for 25 minutes. Remove cover and sprinkle chow mein noodles over top. Bake 5 minutes longer. *Serves 4 to 6*

MICROWAVE METHOD:
Prepare as above. Cook on high for 6 to 8 minutes. Sprinkle chow mein noodles over top. Cook on high 1 to 2 minutes longer.
Serves 4 to 6

Chicken Chop Suey

1 cup diagonally sliced celery
1 medium onion, sliced
3 tablespoons vegetable oil
1 tablespoon instant chicken bouillon crystals
1 cup water
1 tablespoon cornstarch
1 jar (2½ oz.) sliced mushrooms
1 green pepper, sliced
1 can (5 oz.) water chestnuts, drained and sliced
1 can (16 oz.) bean sprouts, drained
2 cups cooked, cubed chicken
2 tablespoons soy sauce
2 bags SUCCESS® Rice, cooked

Sauté celery and onion in oil about 3 minutes. Blend chicken bouillon crystals and cornstarch with water. Stir into celery-onion mixture. Heat until slightly thickened. Stir in mushrooms, green pepper, water chestnuts, bean sprouts, chicken, and soy sauce. Cover and steam 5 minutes. Serve over hot rice.
Makes 8 servings (about 1 cup each)

Polynesian Casserole

40 SUNSHINE® HI HO® Crackers
1 cup chopped onion
2 cups cooked chicken, chopped
1 (10½ ounce) can cream of mushroom soup
½ cup water
1 (1 pound) can bean sprouts, drained
1 cup coarsely broken cashew nuts
3 pears, halved and cored

Break crackers into medium-coarse crumbs; there should be about 2 cups. Spread half the crumbs over bottom of a shallow 2-quart casserole. Combine remaining ingredients, except pears, and pour evenly over a layer of crumbs. Sprinkle remaining crumbs over top. Arrange pears on top, cut side down. Bake in preheated moderate oven (350°F) for about 45 minutes or until pears are tender. Time will depend on size and ripeness of pears. Serve immediately. *Yield: 6 servings*

Barbecued Chicken, Korean Style

⅓ cup KIKKOMAN Soy Sauce
3 tablespoons minced green onion
1 tablespoon grated fresh ginger root
1 teaspoon sesame seed, toasted
1½ teaspoons unrefined sesame seed oil
1 clove garlic, minced
¼ teaspoon cayenne pepper
2 pounds chicken thighs, boned
3 tablespoons salad oil

Thoroughly blend together soy sauce, green onion, ginger, sesame seed, sesame seed oil, garlic and cayenne. Cut chicken into bite-size pieces; stir into sauce. Marinate about 30 minutes, stirring occasionally. Remove from marinade and drain. Heat oil in frying pan; add chicken, skin side down, and brown slowly over low heat. Turn chicken pieces over, and cook until tender.
Makes 4 servings

Chicken Subgum Cantonese Style

2 cups raw chicken, cut in small dice
3 tablespoons cooking oil
½ cup onion, diced
1 can CHINA BEAUTY® Chop Suey Vegetables, drained
¼ can CHINA BEAUTY® Water Chestnuts, diced (if available)
¼ can CHINA BEAUTY® Bamboo Shoots, diced (if available)
1 cup button mushrooms
2 cups chicken stock
2 tablespoons CHINA BEAUTY® Soy Sauce
½ cup white wine
2 teaspoons cornstarch
½ cup toasted almonds, chopped
Garnish with pimiento and green pepper (diced or strips)

Fry the chicken in hot oil until lightly browned, add all other ingredients except cornstarch, almonds and garnish. Cover and cook for about 10 minutes. Mix cornstarch with a little cold water, add, and cook until sauce is slightly thickened. Remove from fire and stir in almonds. Decorate with pimientos and green peppers. Serve with steamed rice for Chop Suey, or Chow Mein noodles for Chow Mein. *4-5 portions*

Miniature Chicken Egg Foo Yung

1 package (14 ounces) **Frozen STOKELY'S® Japanese Style Stir-Fry Vegetables**
5 eggs
2 Tablespoons soy sauce
1¼ cups diced, cooked chicken
4 Tablespoons all-purpose flour
4 Tablespoons vegetable oil
Chinese hot mustard
Duck sauce

Prepare vegetables according to package directions and set aside. Beat eggs with soy sauce until frothy. Combine chicken and flour in a small bowl. Add vegetables and chicken mixture to beaten eggs and stir until well combined. Heat oil in a large skillet. Drop heaping Tablespoonfuls of mixture into hot oil to make miniature pancakes. Brown well on both sides. Drain on paper towels and keep warm. Serve with small bowls of hot mustard and duck sauce for dipping. *4 to 6 servings*

Wyler's®

Chicken Cashew

2 teaspoons **WYLER'S® Chicken-Flavor Instant Bouillon** *or* **2 Chicken-Flavor Bouillon Cubes**
1¾ cups boiling water
2 tablespoons soy sauce
5 teaspoons cornstarch
2 teaspoons light brown sugar
¼ teaspoon ground ginger
2 whole chicken breasts, split, boned and cut into bite-size pieces (about 1½ pounds)
2 tablespoons vegetable oil
2 cups sliced fresh mushrooms (about 8 ounces)
½ cup sliced green onions
1 small green pepper, sliced
1 (8 ounce) can sliced water chestnuts, drained
½ cup cashew nuts
Hot cooked rice

In small saucepan, dissolve bouillon in water. Combine soy sauce, cornstarch, sugar and ginger; stir into bouillon mixture. In large skillet, brown chicken in oil. Add bouillon mixture; cook and stir until sauce is slightly thickened. Stir in remaining ingredients except nuts and rice; simmer uncovered 5 to 8 minutes, stirring occasionally. Remove from heat; stir in *¼ cup* nuts. Serve over rice. Garnish with remaining nuts. Refrigerate leftovers. *Makes 4 servings*

Chicken Oriental

3 whole chicken breasts (about 1 lb. ea.), split
2 tablespoons butter or margarine, melted
1 can (20 oz.) pineapple chunks in natural juice, undrained
¼ cup maraschino cherries, halved
1 envelope **LIPTON® Onion Soup Mix**

On heavy-duty foil in shallow baking pan, arrange chicken brushed with butter. Broil 10 minutes or until lightly browned on both sides. Reduce oven to 350°.

In medium bowl, combine remaining ingredients; pour over chicken. Fold foil, sealing edges airtight with double fold; bake 45 minutes or until chicken is tender. *Makes about 6 servings*

Mueller's

Polynesian Turkey and Noodles

2 cups cubed cooked turkey
1 egg, slightly beaten
¼ cup cornstarch
2 tablespoons cooking oil
1 can (13½ ounces) pineapple chunks, drained (reserve juice)
½ cup sugar
½ cup cider vinegar
1 medium green pepper, cut in strips
2 tablespoons cornstarch
¼ cup water
1 teaspoon soy sauce
4 large carrots, cooked and cut in 1-inch pieces
8 ounces (5 cups) **MUELLER'S® Klops® Egg Noodles**

Dip turkey pieces in egg; roll in ¼ cup cornstarch until coated. In skillet, brown turkey pieces in oil; remove and set aside. Add enough water to reserved pineapple juice to make 1 cup; add to skillet along with sugar, vinegar and green pepper. Heat to boiling, stirring constantly. Reduce heat; cover and simmer 2 minutes. Blend 2 tablespoons cornstarch and ¼ cup water; stir into skillet. Heat, stirring constantly, until mixture thickens and boils; cook 1 minute. Stir in pineapple chunks, soy sauce, carrots, and turkey pieces; heat. Meanwhile, cook noodles as directed on package; drain. Serve turkey over noodles. *4 to 6 servings*

Stir-Fry Turkey Roast

½ roasted **SWIFT PREMIUM® Turkey Roast**, cut into ¼-inch strips
¼ cup oil
1 medium onion, sliced into rings
4 ounces fresh mushrooms, sliced
4 ounce can water chestnuts, cut in half (reserve liquid)
½ cup sherry
¼ cup soy sauce
1 tablespoon cornstarch
¼ to ½ teaspoon ground ginger
2 packages (6 ounces each) frozen pea pods

Heat oil in wok, electric frying pan or skillet at medium-high heat. Add turkey roast, onion, mushrooms and water chestnuts. Stir-fry a few minutes or until onions are tender and mushrooms brown.

In small bowl, mix together liquid from water chestnuts, sherry, soy sauce, cornstarch and ginger. Blend well. Pour into turkey-vegetable mixture. Add pea pods. Mix all ingredients well; cover and simmer 5 to 7 minutes. Serve over fluffy rice. *Yield: 6 servings*

TABASCO®
Szechuan Turkey

3 tablespoons peanut oil
2 tablespoons sliced scallions
1 clove garlic, sliced
1 tablespoon minced ginger root or
  ¼ teaspoon ground ginger
1 cup sliced green pepper
2 tablespoons dry sherry
¼ cup chili sauce
2 tablespoons catchup
2 tablespoons soy sauce
½ teaspoon **TABASCO® Pepper Sauce**
1 teaspoon sugar
1 teaspoon salt
3 cups cut-up cooked turkey or chicken
  (cut in ½-inch strips)

In large chafing dish, heat oil over direct Sterno flame until very hot. Add scallions, garlic, ginger root and green pepper. Cook for 2 minutes. Stir in sherry, chili sauce, catchup, soy sauce, **TABASCO®**, sugar and salt. Add turkey; mix well. To keep warm, place over bain marie filled with water, over canned heat.

Yield: 6 servings

Teriyaki Turkey Wings

2 LOUIS RICH™ Turkey Wings
⅓ cup soy sauce
¼ cup sherry
1 tablespoon minced fresh ginger root (or 1 teaspoon
  ground ginger)
1 large minced clove garlic
Optional: 1½ tablespoons grated orange rind

Remove wing tips and use reserve for another use. Cut each wing into 2 pieces at the joint: Place in a single layer in a shallow roasting pan. Roast, uncovered, in preheated 375-degree oven for 45 minutes, until skin is crisp. Drain and discard any melted fat. Combine remaining ingredients and pour over wings. Cover pan tightly with foil and continue baking for another 45 minutes.

Makes six servings, about 300 calories each

Oriental Turkey Stir-Fry

1 package (1 to 2 lb.) **LOUIS RICH™ Fresh Turkey
  Breast Slices**
2 tablespoons oil
1 bunch (1 lb.) bok choy, sliced diagonally
1 can (8 oz.) sliced water chestnuts
1 cup (2 oz.) sliced fresh mushrooms
3 green onions, chopped

Sauce:
1 cup chicken broth
¼ cup soy sauce
2 tablespoons dry sherry
2 tablespoons cornstarch
¼ teaspoon garlic powder
¼ teaspoon ground ginger

Cut turkey breast slices into ¼-inch strips. In wok or Dutch oven heat oil over medium-high heat 2 to 3 minutes; add turkey. Stir-fry 3 to 5 minutes until turkey turns white and begins to brown; remove to plate. Add vegetables; stir-fry 4 to 5 minutes. Combine sauce and pour over vegetables. Add cooked turkey. Heat and stir 2 to 3 minutes more until sauce is thickened. Serve over rice or chow mein noodles.

Makes 6 servings

Turkey Chop Suey

2 cups cut up, roasted, **BUTTERBALL® SWIFT'S PREMIUM®** Turkey
2 tablespoons shortening
1 cup sliced celery
1 medium onion, sliced
½ cup sliced mushrooms
10¾ ounce can condensed cream of chicken soup
¾ cup water
1 tablespoon Worcestershire sauce
1 tablespoon soy sauce
2 cans (16 ounces each) bean sprouts
Hot cooked rice

Melt shortening in skillet. Add celery and onion. Cook only until tender, about 5 minutes. Stir in turkey, mushrooms, soup, water and seasonings. Cook over low heat 10 minutes. For a future meal, pour half the mixture into a 1 pint freezer container. Cool, label and freeze.

Yield; 6½ cups

To serve: Add 1 can drained bean sprouts to remaining turkey mixture. Cook over low heat about 10 minutes or until heated through. Serve over rice.

Makes 3 to 4 servings

To serve frozen Chop Suey: Thaw chop suey mixture. Add remaining can of drained bean sprouts. Cook over low heat about 10 minutes or until heated through. Serve over rice.

Makes 3 to 4 servings

Sweet-Sour Glazed Cornish

4 TYSON® Cornish Game Hens
¼ cup lemon juice
½ cup unsalted butter
¼ cup white wine

Glaze Sauce:
1 cup currant jelly
1½ Tbsp. hot prepared mustard
½ tsp. crushed rosemary
1 Tbsp. lemon juice

Clean cornish with lemon juice, pat dry. Generously coat inside and out with mixture of melted butter and wine. Place on **Spanek Vertical Roasters®***. Sprinkle with salt and pepper. Place in roasting pan with 1¼ cups water. Roast in preheated oven of 450° 15 minutes; reduce heat to 375°F. and roast 30 minutes longer. Meanwhile combine Glaze Sauce ingredients and heat until jelly melts. The last 10 minutes of cooking, brush with Glaze Sauce and brush again after cooking.

Serves 4

*Vertical roasters

PERDUE

Peking Cornish Hens with Scallion Sauce

4 PERDUE® Fresh Cornish Game Hens
6 cups water
¼ cup honey
4 ¼-inch thick slices fresh ginger

Scallion Sauce:
½ cup soy sauce
2 tablespoons sherry
2 tablespoons orange juice
1 teaspoon grated orange rind
1 teaspoon sugar
2 scallions, thinly sliced

Remove giblets. Pat hens dry. Bring water to a boil in large saucepan. When boiling, add honey and stir. One at a time, lower each bird into honey bath, quickly turning it completely over to evenly coat with liquid. Immediately remove and place a slice of ginger in each bird. Let hens dry on metal rack for 10 minutes. Place in roasting pan with wings folded back, but do not tie legs together or truss. Cook in preheated 350° F. oven for 1 hour until tender. Combine Sauce ingredients and serve with hens.

Makes 4 servings

Duckling Quarters, Cal-Hawaiian Style

1 frozen duckling, defrosted and quartered
½ teaspoon garlic salt
½ teaspoon ginger
1 can (1 pound 4 ounce) pineapple chunks
⅓ cup sugar
2 tablespoons cornstarch
¼ teaspoon salt
¼ cup catsup
¼ cup vinegar
1 teaspoon soy sauce
1 medium green pepper, cut in chunks
1 medium tomato, cut in wedges
6 green onions, cut in ½ inch lengths (½ cup)
4 servings hot, fluffy, seasoned and buttered rice
¼ cup chopped macadamia nuts or almonds, optional

Wash, drain and dry duckling quarters. Sprinkle both sides with garlic salt and ginger. Place quarters, skin side up, on rack in roasting pan. Bake in slow oven (325 degrees F.) until drumsticks are very tender, about 40 minutes per pound. While duckling is roasting drain pineapple chunks; save 1 cup syrup. Combine sugar, cornstarch and salt. Add pineapple syrup, catsup, vinegar and soy sauce; mix well. Cook stirring constantly until thickened and clear. Use ½ cup sauce for spooning over duckling quarters for last 30 minutes of cooking time. Just before serving, heat remaining sauce. Add pineapple chunks, green pepper, tomato and onion; stir to coat with sauce. Heat just until vegetables are hot. Serve with duckling quarters and rice sprinkled with macadamia nuts or almonds if desired.

Makes 4 servings

Favorite recipe from **National Duckling Council**

Chinese-Style Pineapple Duckling

1 frozen duckling, defrosted and quartered
1 can (1 pound 4 ounce) pineapple chunks
1 cup unsweetened pineapple juice
2 tablespoons vinegar
1 tablespoon soy sauce
1 chicken bouillon cube, crushed
1 clove garlic, sliced
¼ cup sugar
3 tablespoons cornstarch
½ teaspoon ginger
¼ teaspoon salt
1 medium green pepper, cut in strips*
Hot, fluffy, cooked rice
½ cup chopped salted cashew nuts or toasted chopped walnuts
Cherry tomatoes and watercress for garnish, if desired

Wash, drain and dry duckling quarters. Arrange on rack in shallow roasting pan, skin side up. Cover with a tent of aluminum foil, crimping it securely to edge of pan. Roast in hot oven (400°F.) 1 hour. Uncover and continue roasting until meat is very tender and skin is very crisp and brown, about 45 minutes. While duckling is browning, prepare sauce. Drain pineapple chunks; save the syrup. Combine pineapple syrup, pineapple juice, vinegar, soy sauce, bouillon cube and garlic. Combine sugar, cornstarch, ginger and salt; mix well. Add to liquids and stir until free of lumps. Cook until thick and clear, stirring constantly. Remove garlic. Add pineapple chunks and green pepper strips; heat through. Arrange duckling quarters on rice and spoon sauce over duckling. Sprinkle with nuts. If desired, garnish with cherry tomatoes, cut in half, and watercress.

Makes 4 servings

*Half and half green and red pepper may be used, if desired.

Favorite recipe from **National Duckling Council**

Polynesian Sauce

1 can (8¾ oz.) tropical fruit salad
1 can (6 oz.) **WELCH'S® Frozen Grape Juice Concentrate**, thawed
3 tablespoons honey
2 tablespoons lime juice
2 tablespoons heavy cream
1 tablespoon cornstarch
½ cup water
2 tablespoons grated coconut

Drain fruit; reserve liquid. In saucepan, combine liquid, **WELCH'S® Frozen Grape Juice**, honey, lime juice and heavy cream. Simmer 5 minutes to blend flavors. Dissolve cornstarch in water. Stir into sauce; cook, stirring until thickened and smooth. Add fruit and coconut just before serving. The perfect complement for chicken.

Makes about 2 cups sauce

Sweet and Sour Pineapple Sauce

1 can (8½ oz.) unsweetened crushed pineapple
1 cup chicken broth
¼ cup white wine vinegar
¼ cup salad oil
2 tablespoons soy sauce
2 tablespoons chopped onion
1 clove garlic, crushed
¼ cup **DOMINO**® Light or **Dark Brown Sugar**
3 tablespoons lemon juice

Combine all ingredients in saucepan and simmer 15 minutes. Brush over chicken, spareribs or whitefish during roasting or last 15 minutes on the grill.　　*Makes 2⅔ cups*

Rice & Noodles

Success® Chinese Fried Rice

½ cup diced green onion
1 cup diced celery
3 tablespoons butter or margarine
1 jar (2½ oz.) sliced mushrooms, drained
1 bag **SUCCESS**® Rice, cooked
2 tablespoons soy sauce
1 egg, well beaten

Sauté onion and celery in butter until tender. Stir in mushrooms, rice and soy sauce. Cook 10 minutes over medium low heat, stirring occasionally. Stir in beaten egg and cook until egg is done. If desired, serve with extra soy sauce.
Makes 4 servings (about ⅔ cup each)

Fried Rice

¼ cup cooking oil
2 eggs, well beaten
½ cup green onions cut in 2-inch matchsticks
1 - 1 lb. can bean sprouts, drained
3 cups cooked, unsalted rice
2 tsp. **BALTIMORE SPICE OLD BAY Seasoning**
6 Tbsp. soy sauce
4 oz. can sliced mushrooms, drained, or 4 oz. fresh mushrooms, sliced*
8 oz. cooked shrimp or cooked and julienned pork, beef, chicken or ham

Heat 1 Tbsp. oil in wok or 10-inch skillet. Add eggs, scramble and remove from wok.
　Heat remaining 3 Tbsp. oil in wok. Add onions and bean sprouts, stir fry about 2 minutes. Add remaining ingredients to the wok. Stir fry until heated throughout. Toss with eggs. Serve.

*If fresh mushrooms are used, add to wok and cook partially before adding bean sprouts and onions.

Subgum Fried Rice

½ pound ground pork
1 tablespoon **DURKEE** Instant Diced Onion
1 can (4½ oz.) sliced mushrooms, drained
1 can (8 oz.) water chestnuts, drained and sliced
¼ cup diced tomato
3 green onions, cut in 1-inch lengths
2 tablespoons water
2 cups cooked rice (⅔ cup uncooked)
1 package (1 oz.) **DURKEE** Fried Rice Mix

Brown pork; drain. Add remaining ingredients. Simmer, uncovered, for 5 minutes, stirring occasionally.
Makes 4 to 6 servings

Uncle Ben's®

Uncle Ben's® Fried Rice

1 cup **UNCLE BEN'S**® **CONVERTED**® Brand Rice
2 cups chopped cooked pork*
¼ cup cooking oil
2 eggs, lightly beaten
¼ teaspoon black pepper
2 tablespoons soy sauce
½ cup chopped green onions

Cook **UNCLE BEN'S**® **CONVERTED**® Brand Rice according to package directions. Fry pork in oil until coated and heated, about 1 minute, stirring constantly. Add eggs and pepper and fry over medium heat for 5 minutes, stirring constantly. Add cooked rice and soy sauce. Fry, stirring frequently, about 5 minutes. Sprinkle green onions over top and serve.　*Serves 5-6*

*Diced cooked shrimp, ham or chicken may be used in place of pork.

Oriental Fried Rice

⅓ cup peanut oil
½ cup sliced green onions
1 cup julienne strips cooked ham*
3 cups cooked rice
⅓ cup sliced water chestnuts
2 eggs, slightly beaten
3 tablespoons soy sauce
½ teaspoon EACH: **LAWRY'S**® Seasoned Salt and **LAWRY'S**® Seasoned Pepper
Minced parsley

In large skillet, heat oil and sauté onions and ham until lightly browned. Mix in rice and water chestnuts. Stir in remaining ingredients except parsley; cook until eggs are thoroughly mixed with rice mixture. Spoon mixture into bowl or mold, pressing it down firmly with the back of a spoon. Unmold onto heated platter. Sprinkle minced parsley over top. Serve with stir-fried vegetables.
Makes 4 to 6 servings

*May use julienne strips of cooked turkey, chicken, pork or any combination of meats.

Chinese Fried Rice

8-10 slices of **RATH® BLACK HAWK Bacon**, fried and crumbled
2 tablespoons vegetable oil
2-3 tablespoons chopped onion
2 tablespoons diced green pepper
1 stalk celery, sliced thin
2 cups cooked rice
½ cup sliced water chestnuts
2 tablespoons soy sauce
Dash of hot sauce
2 eggs, beaten

In large skillet, cook onions, green pepper and celery in oil until tender, about 5 minutes. Stir in rice, water chestnuts, soy sauce and a dash of hot sauce. Cook over low heat, 8-10 minutes, stirring occasionally. Stir in eggs, stir-fry 2 or 3 minutes. Toss in **RATH® BLACK HAWK Bacon**, mix well.

Makes approximately 4 to 5 servings

VARIATION:

1 cup **RATH® BLACK HAWK Boneless** or **Canned Ham** may be used instead of **RATH® BLACK HAWK Bacon**. Cut ham into slivers 2 x ⅛ x ⅛ inch.

Hormel Fried Rice

¼ cup cooking oil
1 can (6¾ ounces) **HORMEL Chunk Ham**, drained
4 cups cold cooked rice
¼ cup thinly-sliced green onions
2 eggs, beaten
1 tablespoon soy sauce

In wok or large skillet, heat oil until hot; add ham and cook 2 minutes, stirring often. With slotted spoon, remove ham and reserve. Add rice and onions to wok; cook over medium heat about 4 minutes, stirring constantly to separate grains. (Do not brown rice.) Pour eggs over rice; cook and stir until eggs are set. Add ham and soy sauce; cook and stir until heated and well mixed.

2 to 3 servings

California Fried Rice

½ cup California raisins
4 green onions, chopped
1 stalk celery, thinly sliced
1 cup finely chopped cooked ham
2 tablespoons cooking oil
3 cups cooked rice
3 eggs
1 teaspoon soy sauce

Sauté raisins, onion, celery and ham in oil until tender-crisp. Mix in rice. Make well in center and add eggs lightly beaten with soy sauce. Cook, gradually stirring eggs into rice, until eggs are just set. Serve topped with chopped salted peanuts, if desired.

Serves 4

Favorite recipe from **California Raisin Advisory Board**

Browned Rice with Cashews

PAM® No-Stick Cooking Spray
⅔ cup rice
2 tablespoons chopped scallions
2 tablespoons chopped cashews
1⅓ cups water
½ teaspoon salt
Few grains pepper

Coat inside of medium saucepan with **PAM® No-Stick Cooking Spray** according to directions; heat over medium heat. Add rice, scallions and cashews; cook and stir until rice is lightly browned. Stir in water, salt and pepper; bring to a boil. Cover and simmer over low heat 15 minutes or until rice is tender.

Makes 4 servings

Calories per serving: 128

Pacific Isles Rice

2 tablespoons butter or margarine
¾ cup chopped celery
1½ cups uncooked instant rice
1½ cups hot water
1 envelope **LIPTON® Onion Soup Mix**
1 can (4 oz.) sliced mushrooms (optional)

In medium saucepan, melt butter and cook celery over low heat until crisp-tender. Add remaining ingredients. Bring to a boil; reduce heat and simmer, uncovered, about 5 minutes.

Makes about 6 servings

Rice-A-Roni®
Egg Fu Yung

1 pkg. (6¼ oz.) **GOLDEN GRAIN® Fried RICE-A-RONI®**
6 eggs
1 Tbsp. soy sauce
½ tsp. salt
Dash pepper
1 can (16 oz.) bean sprouts, drained
¼ cup sliced green onion

Sauce:
2 Tbsp. cornstarch
2 Tbsp. soy sauce
2 cups water

Prepare **Fried RICE-A-RONI®** according to package directions; cool. Beat eggs with 1 Tbsp. soy sauce, salt and pepper. Stir in cooked **RICE-A-RONI®**, bean sprouts and green onion. Drop mixture by ½ cupfuls onto greased griddle. Brown on each side.

SAUCE:
Combine cornstarch, 2 Tbsp. soy sauce and water; cook until thick. Serve over Egg Fu Yung. *Serves 4*

Mushroom Almond Rice

1 cup long grain rice
2 cups chicken broth or bouillon
2 tablespoons butter or margarine
½ pound mushrooms, sliced
1 clove garlic, minced or pressed
½ cup **BLUE DIAMOND®** Blanched Slivered Almonds, toasted
¼ cup minced parsley
Salt and pepper

Combine rice and broth in a saucepan and cover; bring to a full boil; reduce heat and simmer for 20 minutes. Do not remove cover. Remove pan from heat and steam another 20 minutes.

Just before serving, heat butter until bubbly in a large skillet; add mushrooms and garlic and sauté quickly. After rice has steamed, add to mushrooms along with almonds and parsley; mix well. Salt and pepper to taste. *Makes 4 to 6 servings*

Top Ramen.

Stir Fry Pork

Before opening break-up noodles in 2 pkg. **Pork Flavor TOP RAMEN®**. Add noodles to 2 cups boiling water. Cook uncovered, stir occasionally for 3 minutes. Sauté 8 oz. thinly sliced pork with 2 Tbsp. butter and seasonings from both flavor packets. Stir in 2 cups ''Oriental style'' frozen mixed vegetables. Cook and stir 3 minutes. Stir in 8 oz. drained sliced water chestnuts and 8 oz. drained pineapple chunks. Toss with hot noodles. *Serves 4*

Oriental Beef Noodles

½ pound beef top round steak, fat removed
1 teaspoon **KITCHEN BOUQUET®**
Sugar
Ground ginger
¼ teaspoon salt
1 package (3 ounces) Oriental noodle soup, beef flavored
1 package (9 ounces) frozen French cut green beans, thawed
½ can (8½ ounces) water chestnuts, drained and sliced
2 tablespoons soy sauce
2 cups water
2 tablespoons sherry (optional)
1 tablespoon vegetable oil

Cut beef crosswise to grain into ¼-inch thick slices. Cut slices into 2-inch lengths. Mix **KITCHEN BOUQUET®**, ½ teaspoon sugar, ¼ teaspoon ginger and salt; add meat and toss to coat. Break up noodles into a large skillet. Add flavor packet, green beans, water chestnuts, soy sauce, water, 1 teaspoon sugar and ½ teaspoon ginger. Bring to boil. Reduce heat and simmer, covered, for 3 minutes. Add sherry and heat through. Turn into 2 large individual soup bowls. Heat oil in skillet. Add beef and sauté over high heat for 1 minute or until brown. Spoon beef over noodles in bowls. Sprinkle with sesame seeds if you wish. Cooking Time: About 7 minutes. *Makes 2 servings*

Cellophane Noodle Recipes

A. Prepare 4 oz. **CHINA BOWL®** Cellophane Noodles*
B. Cut into matchstick shreds:
   ½ lb. lean pork
   2 scallions or 1 onion
C. Mince:
   2 slices **CHINA BOWL®** Fresh Ginger (optional)
   1 clove peeled garlic
D. Mix chow sauce in a bowl:
   2 Tbsp. **CHINA BOWL®** Chinese Dark Soy Sauce
   2 Tbsp. **CHINA BOWL®** Chinese Cooking Wine or dry sherry
   1 tsp. sugar
   1 tsp. corn starch
   ½ tsp. salt
   ¼ tsp. **CHINA BOWL®** Taste Powder—MSG (optional)
E. Cooking: Add 2 Tbsp. peanut or vegetable oil to a wok or large skillet over high heat and, as oil starts to smoke, add scallions, ginger (optional) and garlic and stir fry for 30 seconds. Add pork and stir fry for 2 minutes more. Stir chow sauce and add to wok along with noodles. Reduce flame to medium and stir fry for 2 minutes. Optional: Add ¼ tsp. **CHINA BOWL®** Sesame Oil just before completing cooking. Serves 4 when included in a Chinese family-style meal of 2 other main dishes and rice.

*TO PREPARE: Soak noodles in hot water for 10 minutes and cut with scissors into 2-inch lengths before simmering for 3 minutes in soups or stir frying.

Note: Beef may be substituted for pork in above recipe, but, when using veal or chicken, use **CHINA BOWL®** Light Soy Sauce in place of the **Dark**.

Oriental Chicken

Before opening break-up noodles in 2 pkg. **Oriental Flavor TOP RAMEN®**. Add noodles and seasonings from 1 flavor packet to 2 cups boiling water. Cook uncovered, stir occasionally for 3 minutes. Sauté 8 oz. cooked shredded chicken with 2 Tbsp. butter, seasonings from 1 flavor packet and ½ tsp. powdered ginger. Stir in 1 cup fresh broccoli flowerettes and 1 cup grated carrots. Cook and stir for 2 minutes. Toss with cooked noodles. Garnish with toasted sesame seeds. *Serves 4*

Vegetables

S&W

Polynesian Oven Baked Beans

2 Tbsp. olive oil
3 Tbsp. onion, chopped
2 cans (16 oz.) **S&W® Oven Baked Beans**
1 can (12 oz.) **S&W® Pineapple Chunks**, well drained
1 can (11 oz.) **S&W® Mandarin Oranges**, drained (optional)
1 can (3 oz.) deviled ham
½ cup chopped green peppers
¼ cup **S&W® Catsup**
½ tsp. salt, dash **TABASCO® Sauce**
2 Tbsp. brown sugar

Sauté onion in olive oil until transparent.

Mix in 2 qt. casserole—oven-baked beans, onions and remaining ingredients.

Bake uncovered at 375°F. for 30-35 minutes or until bubbly.

Yield: 6-8 servings

Wok-ie Talkie

1 large head **California ICEBERG Lettuce**
2 tablespoons salad oil
½ teaspoon salt
½ teaspoon monosodium glutamate

Core, rinse and thoroughly drain lettuce; refrigerate in plastic bag or plastic crisper. At serving time, tear lettuce leaves into very large pieces. Heat oil and salt to sizzle in wok or skillet. Toss lettuce with monosodium glutamate in hot oil for 1 to 2 minutes. Lettuce should be heated through but not wilted. Do not overcook. Serve at once. *Makes 3 to 4 servings*

Note: Some experimentation may be necessary to arrive at the exact timing technique to achieve the crunchy "not raw, not cooked, but heated through" results that spell perfection for this dish.

Favorite recipe from **California Iceberg Lettuce Commission**

The Mikado

¼ cup olive oil
2 Tbsp. vinegar
½ tsp. salt
½ tsp. freshly ground pepper
½ cup finely chopped pimiento
2 Tbsp. sesame seeds
1 minced garlic clove
3 cups bean sprouts
1 cup **BROWNBERRY® Seasoned Croutons**

Mix together the oil, vinegar, salt, pepper, pimiento, sesame seeds and garlic. Pour over the sprouts and toss lightly. Chill 1 hour. Just before serving, add Seasoned Croutons.

Stir Fry Bean Sprouts and Peppers

2 tablespoons cooking oil
½ teaspoon salt
1 teaspoon minced fresh ginger root
2 fresh red chili or bell peppers *and* 2 sweet green peppers, cut into thin strips
1 can (8 oz.) **LA CHOY® Bean Sprouts**, rinsed and drained
¼ cup chicken stock
¼ teaspoon sugar
1 teaspoon sherry

Heat oil in wok or large skillet. Add salt and ginger, stirring. Add peppers; cook, stirring constantly, 2 minutes. Add bean sprouts; cook ½ minute more. Add stock and cook, covered, 2 or 3 minutes over medium heat. Stir in sugar and sherry. Serve. *4 servings*

Oriental Broccoli

6 medium fresh broccoli stalks
Olive or vegetable oil
1 clove garlic, split
½ cup thinly sliced sweet red bell pepper
3 green onions with tops, sliced diagonally into ½-inch pieces
2-3 tablespoons **LA CHOY® Soy** or **Teriyaki Sauce**
Salt
Freshly ground black pepper
Toasted sesame seeds

Slice stem part of broccoli thin, discarding tougher portions of stalk. Separate flowerettes. In heavy frying pan, add enough oil to cover bottom; heat until hot. Add garlic and broccoli stems. Cover and cook quickly until partially tender, stirring occasionally. Add remaining broccoli, red bell pepper, and green onions and cook until just tender. Season with soy or teriyaki sauce and salt and pepper. Garnish with sesame seeds. *3 to 4 servings*

Japanese Pickled Cauliflower

1 medium size head of cauliflower
1 green pepper
½ cup very thinly sliced celery
¾ cup **COCA-COLA®**
6 tablespoons wine vinegar or white vinegar
¼ cup sugar
1½ teaspoons salt

Break off each floweret in cauliflower, wash and drain. Wash and remove seeds from green pepper; cut into thin 2-inch strips. In large bowl, combine cauliflower and green pepper. Cover with boiling water; let stand 2 minutes; drain thoroughly. Add celery. In small pan, heat **COCA-COLA®** with remaining ingredients. Pour over vegetables. Toss lightly with a fork, and pack into a 1-quart glass jar. Push down lightly so liquid covers vegetables. Cover and chill overnight. This keeps in the refrigerator for several days. *Makes about 1 quart*

Oriental Cauliflower Medley

⅓ cup **LAND O LAKES® Sweet Cream Butter**
10-oz. pkg. frozen cauliflower, thawed, drained
6-oz. pkg. frozen pea pods, thawed, drained
4-oz. can mushroom stems and pieces, drained
½ tsp. salt
¼ tsp. ginger
⅛ tsp. pepper
1 small tomato, cut into 10 wedges
2 Tbsp. sliced almonds, toasted

In 3-qt. saucepan melt butter. Stir in remaining ingredients *except* tomato and almonds. Cover; cook over med. heat, stirring occasionally, until vegetables are crisply tender (8 to 10 min.). Add tomato. Cover; continue cooking 1 min. Sprinkle with toasted almonds. *Yield: 6 (⅔ cup) servings*

MICROWAVE METHOD:

In 2-qt. casserole melt butter on high (60 to 70 sec.). Stir in remaining ingredients *except* tomato and almonds. Cover; cook on high, stirring after ½ the time, until vegetables are crisply tender (3 to 4 min.). Add tomato. Cover; cook on high (1 to 1½ min.). Let stand 1 min. Sprinkle with toasted almonds.

Oriental Celery Sauté

2 tablespoons butter
2 cups diagonally sliced celery
½ cup diagonally sliced green onion
1 can (4 oz.) sliced mushrooms, drained
1 can (5 oz.) water chestnuts, drained and sliced
1 teaspoon **LAWRY'S® Seasoned Salt**
¼ teaspoon **LAWRY'S® Seasoned Pepper**

Melt butter in skillet. Add remaining ingredients and sauté 2 minutes until crisp-tender, stirring constantly. *Makes 4 servings*

Eggplant Szechuan Style

¼ cup salad oil
1 tablespoon minced pared fresh ginger or
 ¼ teaspoon powdered ginger
2 cloves garlic, minced
¼ pound ground pork
1 teaspoon sugar
½ teaspoon salt
¼ to ½ teaspoon **TABASCO® Pepper Sauce**
1 eggplant, pared and cut into 1-inch cubes
1 cup water
2 tablespoons soy sauce
1 tablespoon sherry
1 tablespoon cornstarch

Heat salad oil in large skillet or wok. Add ginger and garlic. Add pork and cook, stirring constantly, over high heat 2 minutes or until no longer pink. Add sugar, salt, **TABASCO®**, and eggplant. Cook and stir until eggplant is coated with oil. Mix water, soy sauce, sherry and cornstarch, and stir into skillet. Cover and cook 5 minutes over medium heat, or until eggplant is tender. *Yield: 4 to 6 servings*

Hot Chinese Potato Salad

3 tablespoons vegetable oil
4 medium potatoes, halved lengthwise and thinly
 sliced (about 1⅓ pounds)
1 cup *each* carrots and celery, thinly sliced on the
 diagonal
½ cup green pepper strips (¼ x 2 inches)
½ cup sliced mushrooms
1 clove garlic, minced
½ cup water
2 tablespoons soy sauce
1½ teaspoons cornstarch
1 large tomato, cut in thin wedges
⅓ cup sliced green onions

In wok or large skillet heat 1½ tablespoons of the oil. Add potatoes; cook and stir over medium-high heat about 10 minutes until barely tender. Remove and keep warm. Add remaining oil to wok, then carrots, celery, pepper, mushrooms and garlic. Cook and stir 3 or 4 minutes until crisp-tender. In small bowl combine water, soy sauce and cornstarch. Return potatoes to wok with cornstarch mixture. Cook and stir about 2 minutes, just until sauce thickens and mixture is heated through. Spoon onto platter; garnish with tomato and onions. *Makes 6 servings*

Favorite recipe from **The Potato Board**

Sweet-and-Sour Potato Medley

2 slices bacon
2 cups water
1 tablespoon sugar
3 tablespoons vinegar
1 medium clove garlic, crushed
4 or 5 drops red pepper sauce
1 can (10¾ ounces) condensed cream of mushroom
 soup
1 package **BETTY CROCKER® Au Gratin Potatoes**
1 cup thinly sliced carrots
1½ cups frozen green peas
1 cup chopped tomato

Fry bacon in 10-inch skillet until crisp; drain and crumble. Stir water, sugar, vinegar, garlic, pepper sauce and soup into bacon fat in skillet. Stir in potatoes, Sauce Mix and carrots. Heat to boiling, stirring frequently; reduce heat. Cover and simmer, stirring occasionally, until potatoes are tender, about 25 minutes. Add peas; cook 5 minutes longer. Stir in tomato. Garnish with crumbled bacon. *6 servings*

HIGH ALTITUDE DIRECTIONS (3500 to 6500 feet): Decrease simmer time to 20 minutes. Add peas; cook 15 minutes longer.

MICROWAVE METHOD:

Place bacon in 2-quart round microwavable casserole. Cover loosely and microwave on high (100%) until crisp, 2 to 3 minutes; drain and crumble. Stir potatoes, 2¼ cups boiling water, the garlic and carrots into casserole. Cover with waxed paper and microwave 12 minutes. Stir in sugar, vinegar, pepper sauce, soup, Sauce Mix and peas. Cover and microwave until potatoes are tender, 4 to 7 minutes longer; stir in tomato. Garnish with crumbled bacon.

Sweet 'n Sour Fries

½ cup sugar
¼ cup dry mustard
½ cup vinegar
1 egg, beaten
4 cups frozen ORE-IDA® GOLDEN FRIES®*

1. Combine sugar and dry mustard, add vinegar and mix until smooth. Refrigerate 2-3 hours.
2. Prepare **GOLDEN FRIES®** according to package directions.
3. Meanwhile, stir egg into sauce, cook over medium heat stirring constantly until thickened.
4. Serve dip surrounded by hot fries.

Yield: 8-10 servings as appetizer
4-5 servings as side dish

*May also be prepared with the following **ORE-IDA®** Products:
GOLDEN CRINKLES®
TATER TOTS®
TATER TOTS® with Onion
TATER TOTS® with Bacon
COUNTRY STYLE DINNER FRIES®

Tofu-Vegetable Sauté

1 tablespoon HEALTH VALLEY® Safflower Oil
½ cup chopped celery
½ cup chopped leeks or green onions
1 clove garlic, minced
1 10-ounce package HEALTH VALLEY® Frozen Mixed Green Vegetables
2 teaspoons arrowroot or whole wheat flour
2 tablespoons natural soy sauce (Tamari)
1 cup (½ can) HEALTH VALLEY® Chicken Broth, unsalted
1 cup (½ 10-ounce package) HEALTH VALLEY® Hard Tofu, cut into ½-inch cubes

Heat oil in a medium-size saucepan and lightly sauté the celery, leeks and garlic. Add vegetables (no need to thaw) and heat thoroughly. Mix arrowroot or flour, soy sauce and chicken broth, then add to vegetables. Bring to boiling and cook 5 to 8 minutes, or until thick. Add tofu and cook only until heated through. Serve the sauté over cooked **HEALTH VALLEY® Elbow Pasta** for a complete meal. Total Preparation Time: 20 minutes.

Yield: 4 servings

Oriental Stir-Fry Vegetables

¼ cup soy sauce
1 teaspoon granulated sugar
¾ teaspoon ground ginger
1 cup BLUE DIAMOND® Whole Natural Almonds
3 tablespoons sesame seed or vegetable oil
2 stalks fresh broccoli, chopped
1 green pepper, diced
½ cup fresh mushrooms, sliced
½ cup red onion, chopped
1 cup snow peas

Combine soy sauce, sugar and ginger. Set aside. Heat 1 tablespoon of the oil in a large skillet. Add almonds, sauté over moderate heat until lightly roasted (about 3 to 5 minutes). Remove from skillet. Add remaining oil; heat. Add broccoli and pepper. Stir-fry about 2 minutes. Add mushrooms, onion and snow peas; stir-fry another minute. Return almonds to skillet; add soy mixture, cover and cook 2 minutes longer. Serve immediately.

Makes 5 to 6 servings

Sherried Stir-Fry with Walnuts

1 can (20 oz.) DOLE® Chunk Pineapple in Juice
Boiling water
½ cup walnut pieces
2 tablespoons vegetable oil
1 tablespoon chopped fresh ginger root
1 large clove garlic, pressed
1 medium sweet potato or yam, peeled, quartered and thinly sliced
½ pound broccoli, cut into flowerettes, stalks sliced
1½ tablespoons cream sherry
1 tablespoon soy sauce
¼ teaspoon salt

Drain pineapple.* Pour boiling water over walnuts to cover. Let stand 2 minutes. Drain. Heat oil in wok over high heat. Stir-fry walnuts until crisp, about 1 minute; remove with slotted spoon. Drain on paper towels. Add ginger root and garlic to oil. Cook about 3 minutes. Add sweet potato and stir-fry 5 minutes. Add broccoli and stir-fry until tender-crisp, about 5 minutes. Mix in pineapple chunks, cream sherry, soy sauce and salt. Heat through. Toss in walnuts.

Makes 4 servings

*Reserve juice for beverage

DRY SACK
Chinese Vegetable Stir-Fry

3 tablespoons DRY SACK® Sherry
3 tablespoons soy sauce
1 tablespoon cornstarch
1 tablespoon minced fresh ginger root
½ teaspoon minced fresh garlic
3 tablespoons PLANTER'S® Peanut Oil
2 cups cauliflowerets
½ cup diagonally sliced celery
1 can (8 oz.) bamboo shoots
1 package (6 oz.) frozen pea pods, thawed
1 large red bell pepper, cut into squares
¼ cup PLANTER'S® Salted Cashews

Combine **DRY SACK® Sherry**, soy sauce, cornstarch, ginger and garlic; set aside. Heat 3 tablespoons peanut oil in a wok or large skillet over high heat. Add cauliflower and celery; stir-fry 2 minutes. Add bamboo shoots, pea pods and pepper; stir-fry 1 minute. Stir in sherry mixture. Cook, stirring constantly, until sauce thickens and coats vegetables. Mix in cashews and serve immediately.

SUE BEE HONEY

Sweet Sour Vegetables

2 cups sliced carrots
2 cups sliced celery
1 package (10-oz.) frozen peas
6 small green onions, cut in 1-inch pieces
¼ cup SUE BEE® Honey
¼ cup vinegar
2 tablespoons soy sauce
2 tablespoons corn starch
Salt

Cook carrots and celery in one cup of water until crisp-tender, about ten minutes; add peas and green onions and cook about two minutes, adding a little more water if necessary. Combine honey, vinegar and soy sauce. Add to vegetables and bring to a boil. Thicken with corn starch mixed with ¼ cup cold water. Simmer, stirring, a few minutes. Add a little salt if needed. Serve at once.

Makes four to six servings

Sweet 'n Sour Stir Fry

2 tablespoons oil
1 cup thinly sliced carrots
1 cup Chinese pea pods
1 small green pepper, cut into chunks
1 tomato, cut into wedges
1 cup sliced water chestnuts
½ cup sliced cucumber
¾ cup WISH-BONE® Sweet 'n Spicy French or Russian Dressing
2 tablespoons brown sugar
2 teaspoons soy sauce

In medium skillet, heat oil and cook carrots, pea pods and green pepper until tender, about 5 minutes. Add tomato, water chestnuts, cucumber and sweet, spicy French dressing blended with brown sugar and soy sauce. Simmer 5 minutes or until vegetables are crisp-tender. Top, if desired, with sesame seed.

Makes about 6 servings

Tart Yams

2 lb. yams
¾ cup sugar
¾ cup water
1 tsp. salt
⅓ cup MARUKAN® Rice Vinegar (Genuine Brewed)

Peel yams and slice crosswise about ¼ inch thick. Boil sugar, water, salt and vinegar. Add yams and cook over low heat for 25 minutes or until tender. Sweet potatoes or potatoes may also be cooked in this manner.

Vegetable Egg Foo Yung

4 eggs, well beaten
1 can (16 oz.) chop suey vegetables, drained
⅓ cup sliced fresh mushrooms
3 tablespoons thinly sliced celery
3 tablespoons thinly sliced green onions
½ teaspoon DURKEE Seasoned Salt
⅛ teaspoon DURKEE Ground Black Pepper
2 tablespoons vegetable oil

Combine all ingredients, except oil; mix well. In a small skillet, heat just enough oil to coat bottom of pan. Pour ¼ cup egg mixture into skillet; cook over medium heat until brown on bottom and egg is set. Turn to brown other side. Remove from skillet and keep hot while cooking remaining patties. Add more oil as needed. Serve immediately with Foo Yung Sauce.* *Makes 6 servings*

*Foo Yung Sauce

1 package (¾ oz.) DURKEE Brown Gravy Mix
1 cup water
2 tablespoons sherry
2 teaspoons soy sauce
¼ teaspoon DURKEE Ground Ginger

Combine all ingredients in a saucepan. Bring to a boil, stirring constantly. Lower heat and simmer 1 minute.

Eggs Fu Yung

2 strips bacon, diced
½ lb. green beans, cut into 1-inch julienne strips
5 eggs
2 cups fresh bean sprouts, chopped
½ cup chopped green onion
1 teaspoon KITCHEN BOUQUET®
½ teaspoon salt
¼ teaspoon ground ginger
Vegetable oil
Oriental Sauce*

Sauté bacon and beans in large skillet over medium-high heat for 5 minutes or until bacon is cooked and beans are tender-crisp. Remove from heat. Beat eggs with fork in mixing bowl. Lift bacon and beans from skillet with slotted spoon, leaving drippings in pan and add to eggs. Add bean sprouts, onion, KITCHEN BOUQUET®, salt and ginger. Pour ¼ to ⅓ cup mixture into drippings in warm skillet. Cook over moderate heat, scraping liquid portion to center as it cooks. Turn and cook other side until browned. Transfer to serving plate and keep warm. Continue with remaining egg mixture, adding oil as needed. Spoon sauce over stack of egg cakes. Pass remaining. Cooking time: Approximately 20 minutes.

Makes 2 to 3 servings (8 patties)

*Oriental Sauce

Drain liquid from 1 can (3 oz.) sliced mushrooms into saucepan. Add ⅓ cup water, 1 tablespoon cornstarch, 1 teaspoon KITCHEN BOUQUET® and ¼ teaspoon salt in sauce pan. Cook over medium-high heat, stirring constantly until mixture thickens and comes to a boil. Stir in mushrooms and 2 tablespoons sherry.

Makes about 1 cup

Japanese Stir-Fry Apples

4 apples—cored, cubed about 3 cups cubed
1½ cups pineapple chunks (drained)
2 lb. celery—cut on angle (¾ inch pieces)
½ lb. fresh bean sprouts
¼ cup oil for frying
3 Tbsp. soy sauce
1 tsp. ginger
½ tsp. garlic powder

Stir-fry vegetables and fruits in oil 3 minutes. Add bean sprouts and spices, soy sauce, stir-fry 2 minutes more. Serve immediately—becomes mushy upon standing. *6 servings*

Favorite recipe from **Service Systems Corp.**

Desserts

Domino®

Domino® Chinese Almond Cookies

¾ cup shortening (half butter or margarine if desired)
½ cup **DOMINO® Granulated Sugar**
1½ teaspoons almond extract
2¼ cups all-purpose flour
1½ teaspoons baking powder
¼ teaspoon salt
⅔ cup ground almonds
2 eggs
1 tablespoon water
24 whole blanched almonds

Cream shortening and sugar. Add almond extract. Beat in 1 egg. Sift together flour, baking powder, and salt; add to creamed mixture. Stir in ground almonds; mixing thoroughly. Shape into 24 balls; place 2 inches apart on lightly greased cookie sheet. Flatten to 2½ inches in diameter. Combine remaining egg and water, brush tops of cookies. Place a whole almond on each cookie. Bake at 375°F for 12 to 14 minutes until golden. Cool on racks. *Makes 2 dozen cookies*

Almond Won Ton Cookies

¾ cup chopped toasted almonds*
⅓ cup shredded or flaked coconut
⅓ cup honey
1 teaspoon cinnamon
½ pound square won ton skins
Oil for deep frying
Powdered sugar

In mixing bowl combine almonds, coconut, honey and cinnamon; mix to blend well. For each won ton: place 1 teaspoonful almond mixture onto center of skin. Moisten edges with water; fold in half to form a triangle. Bring opposite points together, pinching edges to seal securely. Deep fry in hot oil (375 degrees F) a few at a time until golden, 1 to 2 minutes. Drain and cool on paper toweling. Dust with powdered sugar. *Makes 3 to 3½ dozen*

*To toast almonds, spread in an ungreased baking pan or skillet. Place in a 350 degree oven or over medium-low heat on the stove top for 5 to 10 minutes (depending on the form of almonds that you are using) or until almonds are a light golden brown, stir once or twice to assure even browning. Note that almonds will continue to brown slightly after being removed from the heat.

Favorite recipe from **Almond Board of California**

Chinese Almond Cookies

1 cup lard or vegetable shortening
1 cup sugar
1 egg
1½ teaspoons almond extract
2 cups flour
½ cup finely ground toasted almonds (see above)*
½ teaspoon salt
Whole blanched almonds
1 egg yolk
1 teaspoon water

In mixing bowl cream lard, sugar, egg and extract. Combine flour, ground almonds and salt; stir into creamed mixture to blend. Shape dough into 1½ inch balls; place 2 inches apart on ungreased baking sheet. Press a whole almond into center of each cookie. Beat egg yolk and water; brush over cookies to glaze. Bake in 375 degree oven 12 to 15 minutes, or until golden brown and crisp. Cool on rack. *Makes 2½ to 3 dozen*

Favorite recipe from **Almond Board of California**

CELESTIAL SEASONINGS® HERB TEAS

Almond Cloud

4 **CELESTIAL SEASONINGS® Almond Sunset™ Tea Bags**
1 cup boiling water
1 tablespoon unflavored gelatin
⅓ cup cold water
¼ cup honey
½ cup undiluted evaporated milk or half and half
3 eggs, separated
½ cup heavy cream, whipped
1 9-inch baked pie shell or graham cracker crust (optional)
Sliced almonds or toasted coconut (optional)

Steep tea bags in boiling water for 5 minutes. Remove tea bags. Soften gelatin in cold water. Add honey to hot tea and mix with softened gelatin. Stir until gelatin is dissolved. Add evaporated milk. Beat egg yolks until well blended. Add tea mixture while stirring. Heat until mixture comes to a boil, stirring constantly. Remove from heat. Cool mixture until it mounds (starts to gel)—immerse saucepan in cold water to speed cooling.

Beat egg whites until fluffy. Fold into cooled tea mixture. Fold in whipped cream. Put into sherbet glasses or pie shell. Chill. Garnish with sliced almonds or toasted coconut.

Asian Almond Float

1 can (20 oz.) **DOLE®** Chunk Pineapple in Syrup
1 can (10½ oz.) **DOLE®** Mandarin Orange Segments
  in Juice
1 envelope unflavored gelatin
½ cup cold water
¼ cup sugar
1½ cups milk
1½ teaspoons almond extract

Chill unopened cans of fruit in refrigerator. In a medium saucepan, sprinkle gelatin over water. Let stand for 5 minutes to soften. Place over medium heat, stirring until gelatin dissolves. Add sugar; stir until dissolves. Remove from heat; stir in milk and almond extract. Pour into 8-inch square pan. Chill until firm (about 3 hours). To serve, cut almond cream into 1-inch squares. Arrange squares in serving bowl; add undrained pineapple and mandarin oranges. Stir gently to mix. Spoon almond cream, fruit and liquids into serving bowls. *Makes 6 servings*

Mandarin Float

Custard:
1 envelope unflavored gelatin
6 tablespoons sugar
⅔ cup **MILNOT®**
1¼ cups water
1 tablespoon almond extract

Combine gelatin and sugar in medium-size saucepan. Stir in **MILNOT®** and water. Heat and stir until sugar and gelatin are dissolved. Allow to cool; add flavor. Pour into 9-inch square pan and chill until firm. Cut into small cubes; float in sauce.

Sauce:
1 cup hot water
2 tablespoons sugar
1 teaspoon almond extract
1 can (16-ounce) mandarin oranges

Dissolve sugar in water. Stir in flavor, add mandarin oranges with juice, and stir. Chill. *Makes about 10 servings*

Lemon Pudding with a Twist

2 envelopes unflavored gelatin
⅓ cup fresh lemon juice
1 (12 oz.) can **DIET SHASTA®** Creme Soda
1½ teaspoons grated lemon peel
2 cups buttermilk
1½ teaspoons artificial sweetener
4 or 5 drops yellow food coloring
Fresh strawberries for decoration

Combine gelatin and lemon juice in blender top. Heat **DIET SHASTA® Creme Soda** to boiling. Pour over gelatin and whirl until dissolved. Blend in remaining ingredients. Pour into serving dishes. Chill until set. Garnish each serving with a fresh berry.

Makes about 1 quart

Kiwi in Pineapple Shell

1 large pineapple
1½ cups strawberries, quartered lengthwise
4 kiwifruit, peeled
⅓ cup sliced, toasted almonds
¼ cup shredded coconut
½ cup **GIBSON Kiwifruit Wine**
2 tablespoons dry vermouth
Sprigs of mint

Slice pineapple in half lengthwise, through crown. Use knife to cut fruit away from both half shells. Trim away core; cut pineapple and 1 kiwifruit into chunks. Combine with remaining ingredients and set aside. Slice remaining 3 kiwifruit and place around edges of shells. Fill shells with fruit mixture. Garnish with mint. Serve chilled. *6-8 servings*

Fluffy Fruit Pie

Crust:
1¼ cups graham cracker crumbs
⅓ cup butter, melted
¼ cup sugar
½ teaspoon cinnamon
½ teaspoon nutmeg

Filling:
1⅔ cups unsweetened pineapple juice
1 package (3 oz.) lemon flavored gelatin
⅓ cup instant nonfat dry milk
⅓ cup cold water
1 tablespoon fresh lemon juice
1 can (11 oz.) mandarin orange and pineapple pieces,
  well drained
⅓ cup maraschino cherries, chopped, well drained
⅓ cup flaked coconut

Topping:
½ cup instant nonfat dry milk
½ cup unsweetened pineapple juice, chilled
1 teaspoon fresh lemon juice
Orange and pineapple pieces, if desired
Maraschino cherry, if desired

Preheat oven to 350° F.

CRUST:
Combine all ingredients. Press onto bottom and sides of a 9-inch pie plate. Bake 8 to 10 minutes. Cool completely on wire rack. Refrigerate while preparing filling.

FILLING:
Heat 1 cup pineapple juice to boiling. Dissolve gelatin in liquid. Stir in remaining ⅔ cup juice. Chill until mixture is partially set. Sprinkle ⅓ cup dry milk over ⅓ cup cold water in chilled small deep mixing bowl. Beat until foamy. Add lemon juice. Continue beating until stiff peaks form. Fold whipped milk, fruit and coconut into gelatin mixture. Spoon into chilled crust. Chill several hours or overnight until firm. About 1 hour before serving, prepare topping.

TOPPING:
Sprinkle ½ cup dry milk over ½ cup chilled pineapple juice. Beat until foamy. Add lemon juice. Continue beating until stiff peaks form. Spread to within 1 inch of edges. Garnish with orange and pineapple pieces and a cherry. *Yields one 9-inch pie*

Favorite recipe from **American Dry Milk Institute, Inc.**

Orange-Blossom Fruit Pie

¼ cup butter or margarine, softened
¼ cup granulated sugar
2 tablespoons brown sugar
1 egg
¼ teaspoon vanilla
½ cup all-purpose flour
¼ teaspoon salt
¾ cup 3-MINUTE BRAND® Oats or
    2 packets HARVEST BRAND® Oatmeal*
¼ cup chopped nuts, optional
1 package (4 serving size) instant vanilla pudding and
    pie filling mix
1¼ cups milk
1 cup whipped cream
1 can (11 ounces) mandarin oranges, drained (reserve
    several for garnish)
1 can (13 ounces) pineapple tidbits, drained

Cream butter and sugars. Add egg and vanilla; mix well. Stir in flour and salt, then oats and nuts. Press mixture into a 9-inch pie plate. Bake in a 350°F. oven for 10 to 12 minutes or till golden. Cool. Prepare pudding according to package directions, reducing milk to 1¼ cups. Fold in whipped cream, oranges, and pineapple. Turn pudding mixture into baked crust. Chill till set, at least 3 hours. Garnish with reserved oranges, and additional whipped cream, if desired.

Makes 1 9-inch pie

*Regular or Cinnamon and Spice Instant Oatmeal can be used.

GEISHA®
Frosted Mandarin Melon

1 11-oz. can GEISHA® Brand Japanese Mandarin
    Oranges, drained
1 large honeydew melon
1 banana, fluted, sliced
Sliced strawberries
1 8-oz. package softened cream cheese
2 tablespoons blue cheese spread (optional)
¼ cup heavy cream
Toasted coconut, slivered almonds or chopped
    walnuts (optional)

Carefully cut peel from melon. Cut top from melon; scoop out inside seeds. Stand melon on serving platter (it may be necessary to slice off some of the bottom, so melon stands level). Fill center of melon with Mandarin Orange segments and other fruits of your choice. Put on melon top. Combine cheeses and cream until smooth and spreadable. Frost melon with cheese. Sprinkle with nuts. Chill about 2 hours. Garnish with more fruit. It is not hard to serve—just cut wedges and spoon on some of the fruit.

Makes 6 to 8 servings

VARIATION:

If you don't want to bother frosting the fruit, just spoon mixed fruit over wedges of melon and top with fluff of cheese; sprinkle with nuts.

Fruit Compote
(Low Calorie)

1 (12 oz.) can DIET SHASTA® Citrus Mist
1 cup diced fresh pineapple
2 cups diced apple
½ cup diced pear
Dash salt
1 cinnamon stick
½ cup diced or sectioned orange

Combine DIET SHASTA® with pineapple, apple, pear, salt and cinnamon. Simmer 5 minutes. Remove from heat, discard cinnamon and add orange. Serve warm or cold.

Makes 4 or 5 servings

Calories: 132 calories per serving

Frosty Fruit Compote

1 can (11 oz.) mandarin oranges, drained
1 can (20 oz.) pineapple chunks, drained
½ cup BOGGS Cranberry Liqueur
Coconut

Mix oranges, pineapple and BOGGS. Place in freezer 2 hours or until fruits begin to get icy. Spoon into individual dessert dishes and sprinkle with coconut. Serve immediately.

Makes 4-6 servings

Tangy Coconut Fruit Dip

1½ cups COCO CASA™ Cream of Coconut
1 can (6 oz.) frozen concentrated lemonade, thawed
    and undiluted
Assorted bite-size fruit pieces such as strawberries,
    pineapple, bananas, apples, pears, melon, mandarin
    orange sections, etc.

In a bowl, mix cream of coconut and lemonade. Stir until well blended. Chill. Place bowl on platter surrounded with pieces of fruit. Spear fruits on skewers or fondue forks and dip into cream of coconut mixture.

Makes about 2½ cups

VARIATIONS:

Substitute frozen concentrated orange juice, pink lemonade, pineapple juice or limeade for a variety of tastes and colors.

Ambrosia Shake

2 cups boiling water
6 LIPTON® Almond Pleasure Herbal Tea Bags
¼ cup sugar
2 medium bananas
2 cups (1 pt.) vanilla ice cream
1½ cups ice cubes (about 9 to 11)
1 can (8 oz.) crushed pineapple in natural juice,
    drained
Flaked coconut

In teapot, pour boiling water over **Almond Pleasure Herbal Tea Bags**; cover and brew 5 minutes. Remove tea bags; stir in sugar and cool.

In blender, combine tea, bananas and ice cream; process at high speed until blended. Add ice cubes, one at a time; process at high speed until blended. Top with pineapple, coconut, and, if desired, additional ice cream.   *Makes about 4 servings*

Frosty Fruit Sherbets

    1 envelope unflavored gelatin
    ½ cup milk
    3 cups cubed cantaloupe
    1 cup **KARO® Light Corn Syrup**

In small saucepan sprinkle gelatin over milk. Stir over low heat until dissolved. Place in blender container with cantaloupe and corn syrup; cover. Blend on high speed 30 seconds. Pour into 9 × 9 × 2-inch pan. Cover; freeze overnight. Soften slightly at room temperature, about 15 minutes. Spoon into large bowl. With mixer at low speed, beat until smooth, but not melted. Pour into 4-cup mold or freezer container. Cover; freeze about 4 hours or until firm. Unmold or soften at room temperature for easier scooping.
                                    Makes about 4 cups

VARIATIONS:

Blueberry Sherbet

Follow recipe for Frosty Fruit Sherbets. Omit cantaloupe. Use 3 cups whole blueberries.   *Makes about 3½ cups*

Honeydew Sherbet

Follow recipe for Frosty Fruit Sherbets. Omit cantaloupe. Use 3 cups cubed honeydew melon.   *Makes about 4 cups*

Nectarine Sherbet

Follow recipe for Frosty Fruit Sherbets. Omit cantaloupe. Use 3 cups cubed nectarines and 1 tablespoon lemon juice.
                                    Makes about 4 cups

Papaya Sherbet

Follow recipe for Frosty Fruit Sherbets. Omit cantaloupe. Use 3 cups cubed papaya and 1 tablespoon lemon juice.
                                    Makes about 4 cups

Peach Sherbet

Follow recipe for Frosty Fruit Sherbets. Omit cantaloupe. Use 3 cups cubed peaches and 1 tablespoon lemon juice.
                                    Makes about 4 cups

Pineapple Sherbet

Follow recipe for Frosty Fruit Sherbets. Omit cantaloupe. Use 3 cups cubed pineapple.   *Makes about 4 cups*

Strawberry Sherbet

Follow recipe for Frosty Fruit Sherbets. Omit cantaloupe. Use 3 cups whole strawberries.   *Makes about 3½ cups*

Watermelon Sherbet

Follow recipe for Frosty Fruit Sherbets. Omit cantaloupe. Use 3 cups cubed watermelon.   *Makes about 4 cups*
                                    (Continued)

Ginger Ale Sherbet

Follow recipe for Frosty Fruit Sherbets. Omit cantaloupe. Use 1 can (16 oz.) sliced peaches, drained, 2 cups ginger ale, and 1 tablespoon chopped crystallized ginger.   *Makes about 4 cups*

Raspberry-Peach Sherbet

Follow recipe for Frosty Fruit Sherbets. Omit cantaloupe. Use 2 cups sliced peaches and 1 cup raspberries.

Steamed Almond Snow Cake

    6 eggs, separated
    1½ cups sugar
    1 tablespoon grated lemon peel
    1¼ cups flour
    ½ cup finely ground toasted almonds*
    1 teaspoon baking powder
    ⅓ cup cold water
    1 teaspoon almond extract
    ½ teaspoon cream of tartar
    Almond Fruits and Syrup (recipe follows)
    Whole natural almonds, for garnish
    Powdered Sugar
    Fruits for garnish: sliced pineapple and oranges,
        grapes and preserved kumquats

In mixing bowl, beat egg yolks until light and pale. Gradually add sugar and peel, beating to mix well. Combine flour, ground almonds and baking powder; add to yolk mixture alternately with water and extract. In separate bowl, beat egg whites until foamy; add cream of tartar; beat to soft peaks. Fold whites into yolk mixture. Pour batter into waxed paper-lined 8 to 10-cup mold. Set a wire rack in the bottom of a large kettle or Dutch oven with lid. Fill with about 1 inch boiling water. Set mold on rack, cover with lid and steam over medium heat 30 to 40 minutes, or until pick inserted in center of cake comes out clean. Meanwhile, prepare Almond Fruits and Syrup; set aside. Cool cake in mold 10 minutes before removing and gently peeling off paper. Set cake on serving dish with rim. Slowly pour Almond Syrup over cake, allowing it to soak in. Just before serving, garnish cake with whole almonds; dust with powdered sugar. Surround with poached fruits and fruits for garnish.   *Makes one cake, about 8 to 10 servings*

Almond Fruits and Syrup

    1 cup sugar
    ¾ cup water
    1½ tablespoons grated fresh ginger
    ⅓ cup amaretto (almond flavored liqueur)
    2 apples, cored and sliced
    2 pears, cored and sliced

In skillet dissolve sugar in water over medium high heat; stir in ginger and amaretto. Poach fruits in simmering syrup until just tender; remove with slotted spoon and reserve. Remove syrup from heat; set aside.

*To toast almonds, spread in an ungreased baking pan or skillet. Place in a 350 degree oven or over medium-low heat on the stove top for 5 to 10 minutes (depending on the form of almonds that you are using) or until almonds are a light golden brown, stir once or twice to assure even browning. Note that almonds will continue to brown slightly after being removed from the heat.

Favorite recipe from **Almond Board of California**

Acknowledgments

The Editors of CONSUMER GUIDE® wish to thank the companies and organizations listed for use of their recipes and artwork. For further information contact the following:

A.1., *see* Heublein Inc.

Ac´cent International, Inc.
Pet Incorporated
400 S. Fourth St.
St. Louis, MO 63166

Adolph's®, *see* Chesebrough-Pond's Inc.

Almond Board of California
P.O. Box 15920
Sacramento, CA 95852

American Dry Milk Institute, Inc.
130 N. Franklin St.
Chicago, IL 60606

American Soybean Association
P.O. Box 27300
St. Louis, MO 63141

Angostura International Ltd.
1475 Elizabeth Ave.
Rahway, NJ 07065

Apple Growers of Washington State, The,
see Pacific Kitchens

Argo®/Kingsford's®, *see* Best Foods

Atalanta Corp.
17 Varick St.
New York, NY 10013

Bac*Os®, *see* General Mills, Inc.

Baltimore Spice Company, The
P.O. Box 5858
Baltimore, MD 21208

Banquet Foods Corp.
P.O. Box 70
Ballwin, MO 63011

Best Foods
Englewood Cliffs, NJ 07632

Betty Crocker®, *see* General Mills, Inc.

Birds Eye®—General Foods
250 North Street
White Plains, NY 10625

Bisquick®, *see* General Mills, Inc.

Blue Diamond®—California Almond
Growers Exchange
P.O. Box 1768
Sacramento, CA 95808

Blue Ribbon® Almonds—Continental Nut
Company
P.O. Box 400
Chico, CA 95927

Blue Ribbon Rice—American Rice, Inc.
P.O. Box 2587
Houston, TX 77252

Bob Evans Farm
P.O. Box 07863
Station G
Columbus, OH 43207

Boggs, *see* Heublein Spirits Group

Booth Fisheries Corp.
2 North Riverside Plaza
Chicago, IL 60606

Borden Inc.
180 E. Broad St.
Columbus, OH 43215

Bordo Products Company
2825 Sheffield Ave.
Chicago, IL 60657

Brilliant Seafood, Inc.
315 Northern Ave.
Boston, MA 02210

Brownberry
P.O. Box 388
Oconomowoc, WI 53066

Buddig, Carl, & Company
11914 S. Peoria St.
Chicago, IL 60643

Bumble Bee®, *see* Castle & Cooke Foods

Butter Buds®, *see* Cumberland Packing
Corp.

Butterball®, *see* Swift & Company

Calavo Growers of California
Box 3486, Terminal Annex
Los Angeles, CA 90051

California Apricot Advisory Board
1280 Boulevard Way
Walnut Creek, CA 94595

California Iceberg Lettuce Commission
P.O. Box 3354
Monterey, CA 93940

California Raisin Advisory Board
P.O. Box 5335
Fresno, CA 93726

California Strawberry Advisory Board
P.O. Box 269
Watsonville, CA 95076

Castle & Cooke Foods
P.O. Box 3928
San Francisco, CA 94119

Celestial Seasonings
1780 55th St.
Boulder, CO 80301

Chesebrough-Pond's Inc.
Trumbull Industrial Park
Trumbull, CT 06611

Chicken of the Sea®, *see* Ralston
Purina Co.

Chieftain Wild Rice Co.
Route 7
Hayward, WI 54843

China Beauty®—Great China Food
Products Co.
2520 S. State
Chicago, IL 60616

China Bowl Trading Co., Inc.
80 Fifth Ave.
New York, NY 10011

Christian Brothers®, The—Fromm and
Sichel, Inc.
P.O. Box 7448
San Francisco, CA 94120

Cling Peach Advisory Board
One California St.
San Francisco, CA 94111

Coca-Cola Company, The
P.O. Drawer 1734
Atlanta, GA 30303

Coco Casa™, *see* Holland House
Brands Co.

Colgin, Richard, Co., Inc.
P.O. Box 2158
Dallas, TX 75221

Colonial Club—Paramount Distillers
3116 Berea Road
Cleveland, OH 44111

Colonial Sugars, Inc.
P.O. Box 1646
Mobile, AL 36633

Cookin' Good™—Showell Farms
P.O. Box 58
Showell, MD 21862

Country Pride Foods Ltd.
422 N. Washington
El Dorado, AR 71730

Creamette Co., The
428 North First St.
Minneapolis, MN 55401

Cumberland Packing Corp.
2 Cumberland Street
Brooklyn, NY 11205

Del Monte Corporation
P.O. Box 3575
San Francisco, CA 94105

Diet Shasta®—Shasta Beverages
26901 Industrial Blvd.
Hayward, CA 94545

Dole®, *see* Castle & Cooke Foods

Domino®—Amstar Corporation
1251 Avenue of the Americas
New York, NY 10020

Dore Rice Mill, The
P.O. Box 461
Crowley, LA 70526

Dry Sack®—Julius Wile Sons & Co., Inc.
One Hollow Lane
Lake Success, NY 11042

Durkee Foods
16651 Sprague Road
Strongsville, OH 44136

Estee Corp., The
169 Lackawanna Ave.
Parsippany, NJ 07054

Fisher Nut Company
P.O. Box 43434
St. Paul, MN 55164

Florida Department of Citrus
1115 E. Memorial Blvd.
Lakeland, FL 33802

Florida Department of Natural Resources
3900 Commonwealth Blvd.
Tallahassee, FL 32303

French, R. T., Co.
One Mustard Street
Rochester, NY 14609

Geisha®—Nozaki America, Inc.
1 World Trade Center
New York, NY 10048

General Mills, Inc.
P.O. Box 1113
Minneapolis, MN 55440

Gerber Products Company
445 State Street
Fremont, MI 49412

Gibson Wine Company
P.O. Drawer E
Elk Grove, CA 95624

Golden Grain Macaroni Co.
1111-139th Avenue
San Leandro, CA 94578

Grandma's®—Duffy-Mott Co., Inc.
370 Lexington Ave.
New York, NY 10017

Gravymaster Inc.
599 Connecticut Ave.
Norwalk, CT 06854

Gulf and South Atlantic Fisheries
Development Foundation
5401 W. Kennedy Blvd.
Tampa, FL 33609

Harvest Brand®, *see* National Oats
Company Inc.

Health Valley Natural Foods
700 Union Street
Montebello, CA 90640

Heinz U.S.A.
P.O. Box 57
Pittsburgh, PA 15230

Heublein Inc.
Grocery Products Group
Farm Springs Road
Farmington, CT 06032

Heublein Spirits Group
330 New Park Avenue
Hartford, CT 06101

High Liner®—National Sea Products Ltd.
555 Burnham Thorpe Rd.
Etobicoke, Ontario
Canada M9C 2Y3

Hillshire Farm®, *see* Kahn's and Company

Holland House Brands Co.
P.O. Box 336
Ridgefield, NJ 07657

Hormel, Geo. A., & Co.
P.O. Box 800
Austin, MN 55912

Irish Mist®, *see* Heublein Spirits Group

Jeno's
525 Lake Avenue South
Duluth, MN 55802

Jimmy Dean Meat Company, Inc.
1341 W. Mockingbird Ln.
Dallas, TX 75247

John Morrell & Co.
191 Waukegan Rd.
Northfield, IL 60093

Kahn's and Company
3241 Spring Grove Ave.
Cincinnati, OH 45225

Karo®, *see* Best Foods

Kikkoman International, Inc.
P.O. Box 784
San Francisco, CA 94101

Kingsford's®, *see* Best Foods

Kitchen Bouquet®—Clorox Company
P.O. Box 24305
Oakland, CA 94623

Kretschmer—International Multifoods
Box 2942
Minneapolis, MN 55402

Kubla Khan Food Co.
P.O. Box 42222
Portland, OR 97242

La Choy Food Products
Stryker Street
Archbold, OH 43502

La Sauce®—Armour and Company
111 W. Clarendon
Phoenix, AZ 85077

Land O'Lakes, Inc.
P.O. Box 116
Arden Hills, MN 55440

Lawry's Foods, Inc.
570 West Avenue 26
Los Angeles, CA 90065

Lea & Perrins, Inc.
1501 Pollitt Drive
Fair Lawn, NJ 07410

Leafy Greens Council
503 S. Oak Park Avenue
Oak Park, IL 60304

Lipton, Thomas J., Inc.
800 Sylvan Avenue
Englewood Cliffs, NJ 07632

Louis Rich Company
Div. of Oscar Mayer Foods Corp.
P.O. Box 7188
Madison, WI 53707

Marukan Vinegar (U.S.A.) Inc.
7755 E. Monroe St.
Paramount, CA 90723

Mazola®, *see* Best Foods

Merlino Macaroni Co.
8247 South 194th St.
Kent, WA 98032

Milnot Company
P.O. Box 190
Litchfield, IL 62056

Mrs. Paul's Kitchens, Inc.
5830 Henry Avenue
Philadelphia, PA 19128

Mueller, C. F., Company
180 Baldwin Avenue
Jersey City, NJ 07306

National Duckling Council
503 S. Oak Park Avenue
Oak Park, IL 60304

Index